MW01292289

BEHIND
the SCENES

My Process to Prosperity,
Wealth, Health, and Wholeness

Antonette Smith

PAGE PUBLISHING, INC.
New York, NY

First originally published by Page Publishing, Inc. 2019

ISBN 978-1-64462-598-9 (Paperback)
ISBN 978-1-64462-599-6 (Digital)

Printed in the United States of America

To all my audience of *The Real Antonette Come Forth* book series, thank you for your support of the series. Because of your desire for realness and truth, I was able to share my life story with you. I told my story as a testimony of God's grace and mercy toward me. I told my story so you can witness the power of God at work in me and my life. The power of the blood of Jesus and what He died for me to have and to give me. The gift of the Holy Spirit who really is the one who takes me into the deep things of God. I pray I have been a blessing to you and your families. I pray you have gained the courage to deal with the hurts of your past, to embrace your present, and prepare for your future through Jesus Christ our Lord.

Contents

Preface

Behind the Scenes: My Process to Prosperity, Wealth, Health, and Wholeness is the beginning of the five-book sequel to *The Real Antonette Come Forth* series. In this five-book sequel, I deal more with the emotional and mental journey of my life. The real effects of not telling I was molested. The continual abuse I endured for my entire life until a few years ago. I didn't get free from everything all at once. I had to work through each area of my life—each form of abuse one at a time. I had to get delivered from the physical abuse first and foremost before I could begin in any other area.

After the physical abuse was somewhat subdued, and I say somewhat because it would reoccur periodically. I tacked the drug abuse, then my sexual addiction. Not sexual abuse yet, but addiction as a result of my early molestation and rape. I addressed the emotional and mental abuse during each process to deliverance in each area.

I start the sequel with *Behind the Scenes* so you will have an understanding of my process in which how I got to the place I am in life today. The route I took to become free, whole, and sound in mind and body. There are probably hundreds of ways to obtain easily what I gained the hard way, but this is my process, my life path, and the road God choose for me that was necessary for my growth and development to be fully used by Him in every area of my life, to give Him complete control of me and my life. And I'm so grateful God is good, and He knows what is best for me and plans my life from my end to my beginning.

I am truly a wonderful, gracious, beautiful woman of God. I really truly love me inside and out. I love the real me, the real

Antonette who God created to be. And each day, I discover something new about myself and the godhead over me. I have an amazing life. I'm so humbled and honored God choose me to give the course of life to. He chooses this cross for me to carry. See, we all have a cross to carry in this life. What's yours? Will you go all the way like Jesus to Calvary? Or will you stay in the garden and conform to your own will and settle? I choose to go all the way to Calvary and be killed, resurrected by God Himself to walk and live in newness of life (Romans 6, KJV).

Book 2 titled, *After the Pain: The Dangers of Good Desires at the Wrong Time for the Wrong People.* Of this sequel, I deal with my relationships with men. The hardships I faced in my love life and disappointments with love. Heartbreaks without ever having true intimacy.

Book 3 titled, *My Life as a Caregiver: How I Became the Best in My Field.* Of the sequel deals with my journey to my passion, pleasure, purpose in life that lead to the career path that would take me places I never dreamed I would go, around with people I never expected to meet, and joy and happiness I never imagined.

Book 4 titled, *The Heart of the Matter: God Cleansing My Insides and Facing the Truth about Myself.* Of this sequel deals with all the evil I held in my heart toward my abusers, family, friends, people, even myself. I lived a life of falseness in every area because I wasn't the real me. So I had to face my own reality that I wasn't the nice girl people thought I was, or I had not become the good mother I planned to be. I lied about being faithful to my spouse, my boss, my pastor, and all involved in this mess called life I was stuck in. I say stuck in because it wasn't living by any means. I don't even call it existing because to exist, you must be current. I was stuck at age five all my life even though I was married, birth five children, and being a somewhat productive human being to a certain degree.

Book 5, *Made for Him: God Uniquely Made Me for My Husband.* God made and built me to be exactly what my husband needed and wanted. I had to be processed out of a lot of things spiritually, mentally, physically, and emotionally before I could be joined to my soul mate—the man I was created for. God had to teach me to be faithful first, to be loyal, to be honest, to be a friend, to be a helpmeet, and to be a wife. This process has taken, is taking years. I take one day at a time and try not to rush this process or God because I desire a real mate. But I have chosen to complete my process, and in God's timing, my king will find me. We will meet at the appointed time, and I will fit right at His side because there is where I was taken from to be presented as a gift to Him.

Welcome to *Behind the Scenes*

This sequel will be even more real, in-depth, and brutally honest than *The Real Antonette Come Forth* series because I have exposed all my past issues, secrets, and pains. I walk in the truth of who I am today, not who I used to be or the situations that altered my life. I am living in true freedom in every area of my life. Enjoy the beginning of this sequel that continues to unfold my life page by page.

*C*hapter 1

The Word of God

Hebrews 4:12 (KJV) says, "For the word of God is quick, and powerful, and sharper than any two-edged sword, piercing even to the dividing asunder of the soul and spirit, and of the joints and marrow, and is a discerner of the thoughts and intents of the heart."

In order to begin your process toward any goal or dream, you have to establish a foundation. What is a foundation? Foundation is the lowest load-bearing part of a building typically below ground level. An underlying basis or principle for something (*Webster*).

A proper foundation does more than just hold a house above ground, it also keeps out moisture, insulates against the cold, and resists movement of the earth around it, and it should last forever.

This is my foundation to prosperity, wealth, health, and wholeness I build to stand on. I didn't build my foundation out of anything and everything, but I choose to build on the Word of God. I choose to keep it simple and not overwhelm myself with learning and memorizing a lot of scriptures. I had already learned a lot of scriptures as a child through Bible Witness Camp in Hopkins Park, Illinois, at Awana Camp but as you study and listen to the Word of God, you will remember. This one principle has kept me my entire life through sin, drugs, and abuse. I was taught as a child that the Word of God will stand any test and survive anything. I set to build a solid foundation with the Word of God, but before you can build your foundation, you must understand the building plans and is your goal connected to God's will for your life.

There is concern requires to obtaining the promises of God. God has His own way of doing things, and you have to follow His plan to get what He has. It depends on you how fast or slows your process will be or take. It took me over twenty-five years to achieve or breakthrough to my goals and dreams. Mainly because of my pride, stubbornness, lack of trust, being headstrong, self-willed, and independent were my strongest bonds to break and roads to close. I achieved much small success on the way to freedom. But I took many dead-end roads because of pride made multiple U-turns because of disobedience. I entered several roadblocks that said "Do Not Enter Because of Impatience" and went under construction by the Holy Ghost for trying to do things my way and by myself.

Independence is a very strong and deadly spirit that lead me to stop sign after stop sign. Hatred caused me to walk alone on high-ways. Unforgiveness took me on whining roads that lead back to my starting point. Avoidance was the dump truck I carried for years. Love or hate was always my four-way stop signs. I was glad to see my railroad crossing that meant rest and relax for a minute on my jour-ney. But the speed limit decreased from sixty to fifty-five to long red lights for me to pause and think about my next decision. This is the roads of decisions and choices. I'll tell you more about my journey in the coming chapters. You must die to yourself and learn of and from others to be free in any area. I pray your process will not take as long as mine. Allow me to help speed up your process to change, to freedom, to prosperity, health, wealth, and wholeness.

Foundation Scriptures for My Process

1. Joshua 1:8 (KJV) says, "This book of the law shall not depart out of your mouth; but thou shalt meditate therein day and night that thou mayest observe to do according to all that is written therein: for then thou shalt make thy way prosperous, and then thou shalt have good success."

My Interpretation of This Scripture

This scripture is telling me to speak what I read in this book of the law, which is the Word of God. I should only say what God has said. I am supposed to meditate, stop, think deeply, slow down, and consider what God has said in His word toward me. Once I meditate on this Word day and night, I can properly apply it to my daily life. It says that I mayest observe to do, mean read to learn instructions, seek His ways and process of doing things according to all that is written that tells me that every answer I need for a situation in my life past, present, or future can be found in the Word of God.

Once I have found the method, the answer, the instructions for the change of my situation or circumstances and apply it to my daily life, then and only then can I make my way prosperous and have good success. If I try any other way, if I might bring temporary relief or change but not lasting effect and change.

2. Proverbs 18:21 (KJV) says, "Death and life are in the power of the tongue: and they that love it shall eat the fruit thereof."

My Interpretation of This Scripture

This is the most powerful scripture I think I have ever read and understood that bought immediate conviction, change, correction, and remorse to me all at the same time. I realized that I had created a lot of the problems I was facing in my life by simply saying negative things out loud, speaking of gloom and doom in my daily speech, cursing and swearing, cursing others and myself with my mouth, my words. You speak life, and you speak death. After I gained revelation knowledge of this scripture, it was hard for me to say I was this and that.

Example, I was ordered at age twenty-two to go to in-house rehab for drug addiction for twenty-eight days. Well, part of alcohol anonymous (AA) and (NA) narcotic anonymous is you have to admit out loud you are an addict and state your drug of choice. Well, when it came to my turn, I said, "Hello, my name is Antonette," and I sat down.

My counselor said, "You have to finish the sentence like everyone else."

I said, "I hold the power of life and death in my tongue, and I will only say what God has said about me."

They wrote me up, and I had to go to a council meeting. He told me I was in denial about my addiction and what got me to rehab. He said I would never recover unless I accept responsibility for my own actions and talk about my past and secrets. I told him I will never sit in a group of strangers and tell my business to a group of people that's worse than me. I didn't ask to come there I was ordered to come. I told him I wasn't homeless, begging, or borrowing to support my drug habit and that I could stop when I got ready like I did before without rehab or him and walked out. Well, because of my mouth, they took many privileges from me, and I still refused to say I was an addict. I knew I only had twenty-eight days to be there. Well, years later, as my addiction got the best of me, I had to accept that I was an addict not only of drugs but of many things. I explain more in chapter 2 titles "Honesty." This was a part of becoming honest with myself, not so much about words or speech.

3. Psalms 1:1–3 (KJV) says, "Blessed is the man that walketh not in the counsel of the ungodly, nor standeth in the way of sinners, nor sitteth in the seat of the scornful. But his delight is in the law of the Lord; and in his law doth he meditates day and night. And he shall be like a tree planted by the rivers of water, that bringeth forth his fruit in his season; his leaf also shall not wither; and whatsoever he doeth shall prosper."

My Interpretation of These Scriptures

This passage of scripture deals with three postures. Walketh, sitteth, and standeth means to be continuing movements.

A. You will be blessed if you walk with people that are blessed and wise, not people of low degree or not in Christ ways of life. You have to continue to walk and grow and learn new ways of Christ.

B. Standeth in the way of sinners means to stand around people that do not seek or have a desire to know Christ or His ways. People that give themselves over to the works of the flesh—smoking, drinking, gambling, drugs, fornication, killings, or hatred.

C. Sitteth in the seat for the scornful. People who have derision in their hearts for the things of God, they take lightly things of God, they push them aside as if they mean nothing, mocking Him and His people, making remarks to belittle them, looking down on people, expressing an attitude of contempt toward someone.

D. He delights himself in the laws of the Lord, meaning you love and enjoys the Word of God, believes the Word of God, he sits down and study and meditate, think deeply about the Word of God day and night.

E. He shall be like a tree planted by the rivers of water, meaning once you surround yourself with blessed people that are living in the ways of God and don't stand around sinners that disregard God and His ways and avoid sitting in the seat of the scornful, the mean, the hateful attitudes of derision, then meditate, think, and study the Word of God day and night, then and only then shall you be like a tree planted.

A tree has roots. Some shallow, some deep like the roots in redwoods and sequoia trees grow to twenty to twenty-six feet tall. Their roots had to be deep to sustain the growth and height of the tree height. The Word of God is your roots and foundation. This makes you a tree, steady and strong no matter what storms rise or winds may blow. You may bend, but you will not break or be destroyed.

F. You will be planted by waters, which makes you grow, refreshes you, revive, and replenish you.

G. Shall bring forth fruit in His season, and His leaf shall not wither, and whatsoever he doeth shall prosper, meaning there is a set time and season for your prosperity in God. Your leaf is your work, your labor of love, your preparation for prosperity, wealth, health, and wholeness will come to pass. It's a promise.

H. Once you are rooted in God, whatever you do you will prosper. Whatsoever implies that if I choose to be wealthy, I will succeed, if I choose to be healthy, I will be, if I choose to be married, single, I will be. If I choose to create multiple companies, raise children, serve the poor, I will do it because whatsoever I do after getting rooted in God, He has promised to prosper the works of my hands. And I had the keys to unlock the future and life I desire to have and live.

My goal was to live a life of prosperity, wealth, health, and wholeness. But I had to define what each of them was that I might set my aim to conquer these specific areas. It's imperative that you are clear in your goals, your aim, and your targets. If you are unclear in what you want, you will set out to search any or everything or nothing. Vision is vital to this process. What do you hope to gain at the end of your process? What do you define as your dream life? What does your future look like to you? Do you even have a vision for your future? Vision for your family? Vision for your mate? Vision for your children? Vision for your grandchildren? Where do you see yourself at age twenty, thirty, forty, fifty, sixty, and beyond? These were all the questions I would ask myself as I cried myself to sleep many nights, wondering will I ever really feel love—real love, wishing God would just wake me up out this nightmare of a life I had. Some of this life was dealt with me by other people. Some were passed down through my bloodline of my parents and grandparents, and some I created myself. Either way it went, I was stuck with my mess and their mess too, and it all was heavy, it all was toxic, and it all was killing me.

Year after Year

I began to remember all the different Bible scriptures I would quote as a child at Bible Witness Camp. Even throughout my life, I never forgot those scriptures. Many would pop up in my head as I cried and prayed and suffered from depressions of many sorts. I decided that I was gonna give God a chance to really work in my life, so I began the process of seriously reading and studying the Word of God because He said in Matthew 24:35 (KJV), "The heaven and earth shall pass away, but my words shall never pass away."

As I began to take the Word of God seriously and attend Bible studies to better understand the scriptures I was reading, I began to go to the library to research different scriptures in Greek and Hebrew. I used a *Webster Dictionary* and strong concordance for deeper under-standing. I began to purchase many different audio sermons from varies preachers on different topics and subjects. I read many books on the topics I choose to conquer. I kept a journal, always to write about my days when I arose and when I lay down. I listened to music that would soften my heart and made me fill with love and emotions that would lift my spirits from the dump, so I didn't listen to rap, hard-core music that went against my process in any way. As the Word of God was beginning to become real to me, and I learned how to apply scriptures to my life, I set in on my goals and searched for scriptures to help me achieve them. I studied other men and women lives that where I was trying to go.

After months of reading and searching scriptures, I realized that Jesus still loved me beyond my faults, that He was for me and died that I might have life and have life more abundantly. But what did that mean to have a life? To be born again or what? More abundantly, what was that all about? He wishes above all things that thou mayest prosper and be in health even as thy soul prospers. What was pros-per? And what does my soul have to do with being in health? See, I questioned these scriptures and words and wanted to understand what was God really saying to me. So I began to define my words for my process.

This Is the True Meaning of Prosperity

Prosperity—a successful, flourishing, or thriving condition, especially in financial respects; good fortune (*Webster*).

Prosperity—according to the strong complete concordance of the Bible, one Hebrew word for *prosperity* is "shalom." Blessings and prosperity are more than money. We often associate the word shalom with peace, but the peace Christ went to war for on the cross is a "complete, whole kind of peace." It represents completeness, soundness, welfare, and peace. It represents completeness in number and safely and soundness in your physical body. Shalom also covers relationships with God and with people.

I learned that God's thoughts concerning prosperity are much higher than you can ever imagine. God's desire is to bless you and prosper you, two different words, two different meanings, two different assignments. See, we wrap prosperity in the blanket of money, and God has said its more than money, it flows into the realm of favor means grace, His protection favor that affords you joy, pleasure, delight, sweetness, charm, loveliness, goodwill, benefit, bounty, and reward. God's kindness and benevolence have given to those that love Him. Favor releases great blessings, including prosperity, health, and opportunities for advancement. When you have God's favor, blessing, and prosperity on you, it causes you to experience many breakthroughs.

This Is the True Source and Plan of Obtaining Wealth

Wealth—an abundance of valuable possessions or money. The state of being rich; material prosperity. Plentiful supplies of a particular resource (*Webster*).

Wealth—God's point of view apart from the benevolence of God, we are unable to amass wealth. While our labor, planning, diligence, and wisdom are vital, God remains the source of blessing. God is our fountainhead of life, health, wealth, food, sun, and all the necessary elements needed for prosperity. James 1:17 (KJV) says, "Every good gift and every perfect gift is from above, and cometh down from the father of lights, with whom is no variableness, neither shadow of turning."

Deuteronomy 8:18 (KJV) says, "But remember the Lord thy God for it is he that giveth thee power to get wealth, that he may establish his convent which he sware unto thy fathers, as it is this day."

This Is the True Definition of Body Health

Health—the condition of being sound in body, mind, or spirit. A condition in which someone or something is thriving or doing well. The state of being free from illness and injury. A persons' mental and physical condition (*Webster*).

Health—shalom the stem word means peace and is used in many varieties of expression relating to security, success, and good bodily health. Yeshu'ah means deliverance or help is rendered "help." Literally means healing of the body or Riph'uth. Promoting soundness of the mind and moral character. Arukah literally means repairing or restoring one's health (*International Standard Bible Encyclopedia*).

This Is the True Definition of Wholeness

Wholeness—the state of being unbroken or undamaged. The state of forming a complete and harmonious whole, unity (*Webster*).

Wholeness—the condition of being sound in body. The quality or state of being without restriction, exception or qualification. Not divided or disjointed. Not wounded, injured or impaired. State of being perfectly well in body, mind, soul (mind, will, and emotions), and spirit. Complete sanctification and restoration. God's original plan for man before sin entered the world, and now attainable only through the blood of Jesus (Faithandhealthconnection.org).

Chapter 2

Honesty

Now this chapter is by far the most critical to your life. You process your health, wealth, and anything else you desire to achieve in this lifetime. Honesty, what is it? Why is it so important? Well, allow me to tell you what it is, and why I say it's the most critical part of your life.

Honesty is the steel-reinforced foundation walls and footings made of poured concrete as part of your foundation (ThisOldHouseDefinition.com), that make it strong to support the weight it will carry.

Honesty—the quality of being honest, integrity, uprightness (*Webster*).

Honesty—respectable, decent, of neat appearance, also "free from fraud." From Old French *honesté*—virtuous, honorable, decent, respectable, main modern sense of "dealing fairly," truthful, free from deceit, chastity (Etymonline.com).

You have to become one that will accept the truth and learn the truth and tell the truth in all things. The truth about yourself is by far one of the hardest courses to take because we as human are fickle at best. Fickle—changing frequently, especially as regards one's loyalties, interest, or affection, irresolution, and instability (Vocabulary.com).

We change like the weather and at the drop of the hat. We are so inconstant at times for whatever reasons. But to ask an individual about themselves, many would say all good things. I'm a great man, woman, boy or girl, a good friend, loyal spouse, and faithful to the cause because we think more highly of ourselves than we ought.

Romans 12:3 (KJV) tells, "For I say, through the grace given unto me, to every man that is among you, not to think of himself more highly than he ought to think soberly, according as God hath dealt to every man the measure of faith." We have people think we are good because the career choices and opportunities that we have, the amount of money we have in the bank, the house we live in, the car we drive, where we attended school, what social club we are a part of, what association we belong too, what side of the tracks we were raised on, whom we know, who is our spouse, the clothes we wear, the children you have, whom we help, whom we gave money to, whom we befriended, who knows us.

Many define themselves according to those list of things though they are a list of great things, ideas, and trues that are important to a certain degree because many of them bring you pride if mixed with the wrong attitude of the heart. We have to be honest with ourselves in every area to become authentically and genuinely the person God has called us to be. Operate in true humility and respect for all mankind.

Lack prejudice on every level. Honesty is an attitude of the heart. It's a part of you, your character that many lacks for whatever reasons. Most are not honest with themselves about their faults or character defects because we want to appear strong like we have it all together. We are in control and don't have a past or history. Well, as for me, I had to accept some hard trues about myself and be totally honest before the Lord to become free in every area of my life, and it was hard because I really thought I was a good person with just a few secrets because I helped many children and families, I paid my tithes at church, I housed many homeless, I cooked and fed hundreds of thousands of people in my lifetime. I never belittled anyone but accept all who crossed my path. I never intentionally hurt anyone, and I tried hard to learn a good way of life and love people, and I took great pride in all my acts of service and outreach to many until I went before the Lord to get free from my past, and He began to talk to me about myself with this scripture.

Isaiah 64:6 (KJV) says, "But we are all unclean thing, and all our righteousness are as filthy rags; and we all do fade as a leaf; and our iniquities, like the wind, have taken us away." I almost fainted when I read this scripture in the Matthew Henry version, which says, "They confess themselves to be sinful and unworthy of God's favour, and that they had deserved the judgements they were now under. They refer themselves to the mercy of God as a father and submit themselves to His sovereignty. They represent the very deplorable condition they were in and earnestly pray for the pardon of sin and the turning away of God's anger. And this was not only intended for the use of the captive Jews but may serve for direction to the church. In other times of distress, what to ask of God and how to plead with Him? Are God's people at any time in affliction, in great affliction? Let them pray. Let them thus pray.

This level of honesty takes the grace of God to be at work in you. To receive the total benefits of freedom and deliverance, we have to admit we are nothing and the works we do are nothing without humility, it's all pride and acts of self-righteousness. It's amazing because a lot of my acts of service was taught to me by my father, and I loved to help people, care for them, take care of children, and I love the elderly population. I love to give of myself to certain people and do acts of service for the ones I wanted to be kind to, but my way wasn't God's way. I picked and choose my people and not the ones God sent to me. So I had to acknowledge the sins in my life that I wasn't doing deeds according to God's way. I was living in sin—unmarried but having children, not faithful in any relationship, half-hearted in all I did, not committing to anything fully or anyone, lying, stealing, using drugs and selling them, falsely accusing others of my wrongs, a heart of hatred toward my molesters, bitterness toward my children's fathers because of their lack of involvement, mounts of anger toward my parents for not noticing that I was molested from age five, hurt from the rejection of my family and being ostracized by my community for getting pregnant at age twelve and having a baby at age thirteen, heartbroken because I felt alone and was alone, hostile because I'm always having to defend myself from people's opinion and abuse from my mate.

I had to accept, acknowledge, and admit all these things were in my heart with pure honesty if I wanted to be healed from my past and set free for my future. I tried to deny the abuse happened on many levels. I tried to smoke it away, drink it away, drug it away, have more sex it away, and not think about it, but it had poisoned my whole being and polluted every area of my life because my foundation and life were built on this bed of defilement, pain, and devastation I experienced as a child.

So the Holy Spirit, which is the spirit of truth, continued to say to me, "Antonette, if you want to be free, acknowledge these things happened to you. Admit you've done something that wasn't pleasing in the sight of the Lord. He knows why you are the way you are and acts the way you act, but that's not the real you. God sees your heart. You have a good heart it's just haven't been handled with care. You desire to love and be loved, but you have to open up your heart and forgive everyone that has wronged you or you think wronged you. Forgive yourself for hurting others because in your hurt, you hurt many. Ask those you can forgive that your sins might be forgiven."

He said when I bring up the things and hidden things of your heart, acknowledge them, repent so we can move on. I said okay. Well, He took me back to age five when my abuse started. I mean to the day and moment it happened. I've seen myself; it was like I'm looking at myself being molested because I was and the feelings I had from that moment on. He walked me through each experience like that, I felt all the emotions, I heard the words being spoken over me as I was abused, beaten, degraded from my abusers, mother, family, ex-husband, and children's fathers, my rapist, and all the people I hurt and mishandled, men I use for my own sexual pleasures.

I cried night after night, day after day because I realized I wasn't as nice of a girl as I thought. I mishandled a lot of people incorrectly. It didn't matter the reason or motive I had for the mistreatment at this point. All that mattered was I confess, repent, and forgive them and myself and learn a new way of dealing with people and how I treated myself. See, one of the biggest, well, two of the biggest issues were I was an abused child trapped in a woman's body and life. I had no self-worth or self-esteem inwardly, but outwardly, I would dress up the hurt little girl day after day, year after year. Press through life hoping for a better day and better way all the time, but I learned you have to actively take control of your own life and create your own happiness and success. When I got that revelation, I began to set ground rules for my life. I would not lie about anything. If my truth hurt someone's feelings or caused a breakdown in our relationship, oh well, because I was determined to be happy, joyous, and free.

When you begin to change for the betterment of yourself, people don't really like that, especially if they are a part of your failing in life or unhappiness. They deem themselves higher than you or above you because you lack something in your character. To make a long story short, people want to control you and control your life, and when you don't let them, they create all kinds of lies, snares, and trap in your path to strategize your demise or downfall. And the people can be your friend, family, spouse, church member, coworker, child. Anyone and everyone are capable of inflicting harm on you at any time or any reason. You just make sure you're true to yourself, and eventually, the people around you will fall in line, or you change company and detach.

Whatever it takes for you to succeed and reach your goal that's what you do for you. I had to do all the above time and time again, but I'm still happy, joyous, and free. Each time I have to change my company and surrounding, I reach new heights, new levels, and meet new people, experience new things, and learn new ways.

Honesty is a powerful force to be reckoned with. It comes from the root word *honor*—high respect, esteem, fulfillment, reputation, recognition, privilege. Remember I told you I lacked self-worth and self-esteem? When I became honest with myself and God, I gained "honor," high respect, and esteem for myself and others.

Chapter 3

Humility

Humility, what a foreign concept in the twenty-first century. Where can I begin to talk about this subject at hand? Well, no better place to start then with me, right? Well, well, let me see I had to be taught humility, I had to be taught humility the hard way because my pride was so high. You heard the American expression, "The bigger you are, the harder you fall?" Well, the higher you are, the quicker and harder you fall. I'm not talking about high in the status of reputation only; I'm talking about high mindedness, puffed up, prideful, conceited, egotism, arrogance, aggressive, disagreeable, being prone to shame, haughty, imperious, overbearing, stubbornness. All these things are a form of pride, opposite of what we are supposed to be. So you can either humble yourself and get the chip off your shoulder, which we never realize or think we had in the first place. Because we are blinded by pride the way we see things, what we think, or what we know or think we know, or we can allow God to teach us humility, or He will humble you Himself. I have experienced three forms of being humble, maybe more, but I'll talk about three because I'm still learning daily the art of humility. First, let's define humility. I don't leave to chance that all my readers know what humility is, so I'll define it for you.

Humility—the having a humble opinion of oneself; a deep sense of ones (moral) littlement; modesty, humility, lowliness of mind (strong concordance). Freedom from pride or arrogance; the quality or state of being humble, low (*Webster*).

Proverbs 16:18 (KJV) says, "Pride goeth before destruction, and a haughty spirit before a fall." The Lord is saying if you operate in the spirit of pride, high mindedness, destruction will be your end. When you are haughty, you are sure to fall. It's clear in God's Word that pride and haughtiness are killers. Why do I call them killers? I'm glad you ask. They're killers because they kill everything in your life, career, relationship, dreams, increase, because no one what's to be around and know it all, mean, and cantankerous individual at any time. They have the tendency to run people away wherever they go, and they are never the problem, it's never their fault, they are good at playing the blame game. But if you begin to just listen to what other people say concerning your behavior and attitude, if you begin to check the condition or motive as to why you do the things you do and how you deal with people with an honest eye, honest inventory of yourself, you will see that you have some form of pride in some area of your life. But you will not see it or accept it as pride if you don't embrace step two "honestly." Now you see how this process is working together, and you need the Word of God to determine what is truth and lie in your life to get started in this process. If you don't have a solid foundation, you will not complete this process correctly. You will be building on rocks or sand, maybe quicksand, who knows. So consider the cost of this process before you begin. You will have a lot of hard pills to swallow as the old folk says.

Now that you have embraced the truth about yourself, you have confessed, repented, and forgave, you see lack of humility in some area or multiple areas of your life and are willing to embrace change to learn a new way, a new attitude, now God can help you and won't reject you. He will hear you now.

James 4:6 (KJV) says, "But he giveth more grace. Wherefore he saith, God resisteth the proud, but give grace unto the humble." Now that you have accepted the truth of the kind of person you are, God can grant you grace to change your ways from high mindedness and pride to humble attitude and humility in every area of your life. I was humbled through pain and sufferings, correction, and rejection because I refused to listen to anyone. I didn't want to be controlled or told what to do once I gained my independence from my ex-husband. But I was wrong in my thinking because I had to learn from someone. You can't learn if you don't listen. You can't grow if you don't learn. How can you learn except you be taught? See, all these things go hand in hand. Nothing is new under the sun, but you won't be under the sun to learn or experience everything, so learn from others that are where you are trying to go. You have to be a student before you can be a teacher. You have to follow before you can lead. How can they hear without a preacher? How can they preach unless they are sent? God has great plans for His people if we would just embrace Him and His plan and purpose for our lives. We will get all He has for in store for us here on earth and in heaven. Stop believing God only has rewards for you in heaven. He has rewards for you on this earth.

Psalms 24:1 (KJV) says, "The earth is the Lords and the fullness thereof; the world, and they that dwell therein." In 1 Corinthians 10:26 (KJV) says, "For the earth is the Lords, and the fullness thereof." God repeated it twice, maybe more than that, but my point is He said it in the Old Testament for the people that only believes the books of the law, and He said the same thing again in the New Testament for those that believe in the power of grace. He didn't change the law or His words, but Jesus fulfilled the law, and the same promises crossed over into the New Testament, which is built on better promises.

Hebrews 8:6 (KJV) says, "But now hath he obtained a more excellent ministry, by how much also he is the mediator of a better covenant, which was established upon better promises." I am telling you take God, at His word, wholeheartedly, build your foundation on the Word of God, be honest about yourself, you faults, character defects so God can cleanse you of all unrighteousness. In 1 John 1:9 (KJV) says, "If we confess our sins, he is faithful and just to forgive us our sins, and cleanse us from all unrighteousness." His promises are not based on your goodness but on His goodness toward you. But our lack of confession and acknowledgment of sin blocks the flow of continual blessings to you. When we accept the truth of who we really are, how we really act toward God, His people, and compare it to Jesus's heart toward us, we have no choice but to fall on our faces in humility because we were born into sin and shaped with iniquity.

According to David in Psalms 51:5–6 (KJV), all of us walk, live, and operate in some kind of sin whether it is outwardly or inwardly. Those inward sins are the ones that kill you in every area. When I was trying to get free from everything in my past, my focus was on my insides what I felt, what I thought. What I thought about people for real, see I was the type I would act one way, and think inwardly about someone another way. I would never say what I really felt or mean to people for a lot of years. I appeared to be nice and friendly on the outside, but I would hate, be full of anger, and rage on my insides, and I used drugs to suppress all my emotions and true feelings of how I really feel and thought. God knows what we really think and feel about Him first of all and then people. God knows us from the inside out. We can fool people, but we can never fool Him.

Jeremiah 17:9 (KJV) says, "The heart is deceitful above all things, and desperately wicked: who can know it?" Everything about you comes from your heart, everything, so God knows it is wicked. He searches your heart. He knows what we are capable of at all times, we don't, but if we humble ourselves under the mighty hand of God, He will guide us into all trues. Humility is a powerful force people of God, powerful beyond our comprehension. When you are humble, you are soft, teachable, you listen, you take instruction, people can guide you, they love your presence, they love to be around you, and they desire your company. But when you are conceited and arrogant, people hate to see you coming, they don't desire anything about you and say to others because most people won't be truthful to tell you to your face how they feel because you are a hothead, quick tempered, and flat-out rude under the belief that you are the nicest person on earth and the most desired, but you are not because nobody likes a hotheaded, a know-it-all kind of person. They know everything about everything and everyone, but they can't pour piss out a boot I heard the older people say that phrase, but they were right.

And if you be honest, you don't like this kind of people either. You might be the person that's not liked. Hey, I've been there. I know how we think of ourselves to be more than what we are. But daily, I humble my own self first and then allow God to send situations and opportunities to assure I stay humble and out of pride completely. That's my main goal each day is to walk in humility. When I master humility, everything else is already in order. Lack of humility takes you out of order, out of bound, on the sidelines, out of God's will and purpose. Well, I pray you to get the picture I'm trying to paint for you. Humble yourself, and God will exalt you. That's my take on humility.

C hapter 4

Prayer

Prayer—what is it? *Prayer* is a word that many people use throughout their daily speech and language. I have heard people use this word so loosely like they were saying hello to someone or good morning as a normal part of our daily speech and form of language. Prayer is one form of worship I take very seriously in my life. I got sick in my stomach when I hear people say or make the comment pray for me or I'm gonna pray for you or you are in my prayers and walk away and never pray for the people or think about their situation again. The phrase "out of sight, out of mind" is what I think when I hear people say this. I respond in this manner because I have a deep understanding of prayer, and it's a form of life for me, and I know prayer has saved my life and kept my mind.

If you say to someone "I'll pray for you," just stop what you're doing and pray for them right at that moment. This is how I respond, and the people will either accept it or not because most of the time, they really don't want a prayer, they want to appear spiritual when they approach you knowing you have a form of godliness about yourself. And the other reason they refuse a prayer at that moment is they just want to use the God method, and I'm praying in attempt to get you to give them something for a quick fix in their life, mainly give them money or a listening ear to tell all their problems too, and they return to their regular lifestyle while you left burden down praying for their situation to change, and they don't do anything to change their own situation or life. So I have learned over the years the true art of prayer and what it is. The biggest revelation of prayer came to me through this book titled, *Lessons on Prayer* by Witness Lee. This book was given to me by Brother David Franklin of Christ Church International when I was sent to him to be trained in ministry. He understood that I was called to be an intercessory prayer. I recommend this book for all Christians, well, all people really because we all pray in some form or another.

My Experiences of Prayer at Different Times, Different Seasons in Different Forms.

Prayer Birthed in Me

At early as age four or five, I remember praying with my mom at night before bed. We prayed before each meal called saying your grace. We prayed at church at Bible Witness Camp. I was told that you could talk to God anytime, anyplace with the method of prayer, and He will always hear you and answer you. So I began my journey of prayer as a child. I remember praying daily and mostly at night after the molestation started in my life. I would lay awake praying. I called it talking to the Lord, mainly Jesus, because His name was the name I heard the most. This method continued in my life.

Midnight Prayer Birthed

I read the scripture in Acts 16:25–26 (KJV) saying, "And at midnight Paul and Silas prayed and sang praises unto God: and the prisoners heard them. And suddenly there was a great earthquake, so that the foundation of the prison were shaken: and immediately all the doors were opened, and every one's bands were loosed." When I read this scripture, something leaped on my insides. I was in my teens at the time of this powerful revelation. This scripture was a twofold revelation to me. It told me that if I prayed at midnight, twelve o'clock, at night, God would move in such and way that the earth would shake. And if I sang praises to Him after, before, or during midnight prayer,

I would be set free from whatever was holding me. This was music to my ears because I was a night owl. Since a child, I would stay awake all night and sleep in the daytime because I had nightmares of my abuse.

And by things time, I was awake with my babies at night. I was on child three when I got this revelation, so my age was about sixteen years old. You read it correctly. I was sixteen years on child number three that I gave birth to. You have to read *The Real Antonette Come Forth* book series volume 2, *The Death of a Girl,* tells about the birth of my first child at age thirteen and volume 3, *Years of a Teen,* to know about the birth of child two and three. So I would pray at midnight and sing a song of praise to God to help me, to move for me in my many situations, which were many at this point in my life. Teen parent of three children, high school student, in an abusive relationship with my children's father, a drug dealer, babysitter, hair braider, having multiple extra sexual affairs and trying to lord the Lord in the midst of this chaos. As you can see, I needed tons of help and from a supernatural being not earthly because I was messed up.

I continued to do midnight prayer for years and still do a lot of the times because it's just my comfort zone when I feel that Jesus is really with me and listening to me and the Father. Now I must be honest with you all. Y'all know I am about the truth and keeping it real. Well, I have always prayed to Jesus in the name of Jesus. Let me explain. I would say the Lord's prayer Our Father who art in heaven. But that would be the only time I addressed the Father in prayer the rest of the time I was talking to Jesus. Until I was twenty years old, and He sent a prophet to me to tell me Jesus was my elder brother, and I needed to address Him as such and pray to the Father God. Well, that roughen my feathers. I was in shock because I thought God, Jesus, and the Holy Spirit were the same person. This messed me up. So I began on this journey to search the scriptures about Jesus being my elder brother and so on and so forth.

Prayer No Matter What Happen or Could Happen Birthed

In my study of prayer and finding out who Jesus really was to me, I ran across the scripture Daniel 6:10 (KJV), "Now when Daniel knew that the writing was signed, he went into his house; and his windows being open in his chamber toward Jerusalem, he kneeled upon his knees three times a day, and prayed, and gave thanks before his God, as he did aforetime." Now, when I read the story of Daniel, I was amazed to see a teenage boy rebel against the king and the laws to remain in relationship and contact with his God through prayer. Daniel did not care if the king would put him prison or kill him. He made a vow to God to pray three times a day and give thanks to him. I'm guessing through singing. You can't really give thanks to God without singing to him as well. So I said, "You know I'm gonna do like Daniel come hell or high waters. I am gonna pray and sing praises every day. It might not be three times, but I sure will do this every day."

I began this method and continue to this day. Even through my years of drug and sex addiction, I prayed and sang to God. I even talked about the holy scriptures while I sat getting high on crack cocaine. The other addicts around me would say, "Tookie, please don't disrespect God and talk about Him, and you're smoking crack." I would say to them, "He knows all and see all, so who you are lying to and hiding from. I know He is the only one that can help me, so I'll talk about Him and to Him when I get ready where I want to and when He's ready for me to serve Him, He will come get me."

And, people, I want you to know that is exactly what happened to me. When God sent Jesus to get me, He snatched me out of the life I was in and put me in another life. I literally went from one kingdom to the next in a second and knew it. It was no denying God snatched me out of Satan's hands and kingdom. I will prove it to you.

In Colossians 1:13 (KJV) says, "Who hath delivered us from the power of darkness, and hath translated us into the kingdom of his dear son." This scripture tells you that you were once in another kingdom before you crossed over to the Lord's side of things and life. I tell you these stories because I want to build your hope, so you will know God has given Jesus the power to come to get you out of and from any situation you are in. I don't care if you are at fault for being in the situation you in. God loves you so much, and Jesus loves you so much He dies so that you can live and life of abundance in love, joy, peace, and fellowship with them and people. If God the Father, Jesus the Son, and the Holy Spirit the comforter and guide can come to get me, deal with me, train me, love me, change me beyond my past, mistakes, faults, and failures, they can do the same or more for you. Just ask them to help you and be willing to confront truth on every level. Be open to change, be open to being taught with new ways, His ways.

4:00 AM Morning Prayer

In 2010, the Lord Jesus sent me to Christ Church International to be trained for the fivefold ministry by Brother David Franklin. How I got to the church was a supernatural work of the Holy Ghost, ordering my steps. You have to read about it in volumes 8 of the series *Birthing Pains*. But when I agreed to join the church to be trained by Brother David who was a prophet that told me words that came from God and showed me in scripture because I was the one that needed proof. I don't just take your word because you say such and such. But God knows how I operate and think, so He got my attention. But during the first few sermons I sat through, he began to talk about morning prayer. Now I already told you I was a night prayer and loved it until about two to three in the morning. Now he was talking about 4:00 a.m. prayer. I will never get any sleep was my first thought. And immediately before that thought was finish, he said, God gives His beloved a rest, pray, God will help you sleep and go to bed early so you can rise early to seek Him.

He used the scripture by David in Psalms 63:1 (KJV), which says, "O God, thou art my God, early will I seek thee: my soul thirsteth for thee, my flesh longeth for thee in a dry and thirsty land, where no water is." He said that if you hunger and thirst after righteousness, God will fill you. My job was to hunger and thirst, and God's job was to fill me. He used Mark 1:35 (KJV), saying, "And in the morning, rising up a great while before day, he went out and departed into a solitary place, and there prayed." This scripture told me that Jesus prayed alone to the Father before He started His day. That caught my attention, but I would pray at the end of each day.

I began to seek God early, search for scriptures concerning morning prayer and purchased books on prayer and fasting as I was prompted by the Holy Spirit.

I read in Lamentations 3:22–23 (KJV): "It is of the Lord's mercies that we are not consumed, because his compassions fall not. They are new every morning; great is thy faithfulness." I began to learn about the mercies of God and when He gives them to us. And if He gives them to us, it is each morning according to scripture. But God said in Romans 9:15 (KJV), "For he saith to Moses, I will have mercy on whom I will have mercy, and I will have compassion on whom I will have compassion." When I got the revelation of this scripture, I said, "Yes, Lord, I will seek you early, and I prayed for my sleep pattern to be changed.

God changed my whole way of life. Everything's changed. Career changed, routine, and lifestyle completely to accommodate God's will for my life, but it was during these years of morning prayer that I was set free and delivered from my past and present. It was in 4:00 a.m. morning prayer where I was introduced to the real me, whom God created me to be. It was during the morning prayer that I learned my assignment in the kingdom of God. It was in 4:00 a.m. morning prayer that I was told what gifts, talents, and anointing I had. This is where I received instructions from God for my life, for my children, for my grandchildren, business, ministry, future, and how to fight the devil.

Private prayer always produces public power. This is the behind the scenes lifestyle I live daily to operate in my daily life. People, I am telling you, if you will seek God early in the morning, your life will change quickly. As I said, I began the 4:00 a.m. morning prayer in 2010, got off course with my times because my life took a shift, and it took years for me to recover. The shift was the hurt of ministry. Ministry hurt almost killed me, almost destroyed me. I know you're shocked I said it. I will say it again. The hurt of ministry from church folks and leaders almost killed me that it almost destroyed me because when you love God, you trust your leaders to love God and care for you and your well-being and some do to the best of their ability.

They really believe they're being lead fully by God in teaching you, correcting you, leading you, and rebuking you, but I had an issue with the correction and leading parts from a few of my leaders because I was going against the will of God for my life and what God had told me personally and confirmed through others. So I wasn't like I was saying, "Well, God told me this and that because I never told my leaders what God was saying to me because you are supposed to be seeking God for instruction in my life, so you are supposed to know my assignment and course of training before I do. But if I know more about my assignment and training process than you, I'm sorry I can't follow you. I can't listen fully to your instructions because they are faulty."

How I know that to be true God has proven it still to this day since my departure from these leaders that I heard Him correctly and to follow Him not man, and He sent to another shepherd that I absolutely love, adore, and cherish, as did the others of my past. Oh, I still talk and fellowship with my former leaders and pastors. I'm not a rebel. I just obey God first and His kingdom. So now since January 2017, I have been under the leadership and mentor of Apostle David E. Taylor of Joshua Media Ministries International (JMMI) of Taylor, Michigan. I absolutely love the apostle and the JMMI staff. The Lord Jesus Christ and the Father Jehovah is working with Apostle Taylor and his ministry. I experience it. I witness it with my own eyes and in my own life.

JMMI is the real deal, the new move of God called *Face-to-Face Appearances of Jesus: The Ultimate Intimacy* is a book Apostle Taylor wrote every human being needs to read this book or touch it, and Jesus will visit you Himself. But since I've been under Apostle Taylor's leadership, he had bought great clarity and healing to my past concerning the hurt of ministry and how to handle it properly and forgive. He explained the 4:00 a.m. morning prayer to me. He has a sermon called "Wings of the Morning" talks about 3:00 a.m. prayer to the breaking of day. God visits man on the earth each morning between 3:00 a.m. to 6:00 a.m. In these times when you pray, your prayer has wings and fly like a 747 jet to be accomplished. I was like wow, I never knew that or heard that, but I knew it was true because

I had experienced it now for seven years when I heard this message. The 3:00 a.m. or 4:00 a.m. prayer will change your life, people.

Different Forms of Prayer

Foundation to Prayer Is Confession and Repentance

Confession—a formal statement admitting that one is guilty of a crime. Admission, acknowledgment, profession (*Webster*).

Confession—Greek word *confess* means "to say the same thing" and then "agree, admit, acknowledge." The context must determine the precise nature, emphasis, and meaning of the word. Thus, it can mean to acknowledge sin or to confess or acknowledge someone as something (Bible.org).

Repentance—the act of repenting; sincere regret or remorse. Remorse, contrition, penitence, regret, shame, guilt ruefulness (*Webster*).

Repentance—Greek word *metanoia* a transformative change of heart; especially: a spiritual conversion," augmented by an explanation of metanoia's Greek source: "from metanoiein" to change one's mind, repent, from *meta* plus *noein* is equals to think, from nous is equals to mind, "change of heart" (*Wikipedia*).

Prayer of confession and repentance are at the heart of the Christian faith. They are at the turning point between unbriefed and brief, and they are the continual reminder to us that our earthly natures are very close to the surface. In the same way that we cleanse our hands by washing as we begin a day, so it is good to remind ourselves in prayer that without the presence of God's spirit in our lives through the day, we are likely to stumble because we are stained by the consequences of sin. Confession earth our lives in the love of God, keeps us humble, and enables us to be a blessing to others through the day (www.faithandworship.com).

Philippians 4:6 KJV says, "Be careful for nothing; but in everything by prayer and supplication with thanksgiving let your requests be made known unto God." This one scripture deals with four forms of prayer. Many people read over this passage day after day and don't grasp that it is telling you did five steps to complete before you reach God. When I began to read about this in Witness Lee book *Lessons on Prayer*, I was amazed. It changed my life.

Step 1: Be careful for nothing—it means to be steadfast, steady, even, and constant in your Christian course (*Matthew Henry Commentary*. This passage is saying to us to be consistent in communicating with God on the daily basis. Keep the lines of communication open.

Step 2: Put everything by prayer—a solemn request for help or expression of thanks addressed to God or an object of worship (Dictionary). This is the method of operation God has designed for us to communicate with Him. This is our only form of reaching God after the fall of Adam is through prayer.

Step 3: Supplication—the act of asking of begging for something earnestly or humbly. This form of prayer is asking and pleading with God for Him to do something for you. I use this form all the time because I am always asking God to do something for me, do something to me, in me, and through me. And many times I have to come back over and over and over because I desire that my request be made known to Him, and He answers. Now I must warn you that I have spent hours, days, weeks, months, and years praying to God, crying to God, pleading with God, begging God, bargaining with God, reasoning with God for Him to answer my prayers that I asked for. I can honestly tell you the most of those times I prayed and cried and begged was I wanted my will to be done, not God's will in my life. Yes, indeed, you read it correctly. I prayed and begged for things God never wanted me to have or wanted me to pray for.

It wasn't mine or a part of the life He had for me. And the funny thing is He gave me most of what I asked for whether it was a part of His part for me or not. He did this to teach me the art of prayer and asking. All the crap and junk the church teaches us about name it and claim it, say it, and it's yours, lay your hands on it, put blessing oil on it, and it shall be yours that is a huge great bunch of crap and mess. Do you hear me? I was claiming other women, men, other people houses and land, jobs, you name it. I probably spent countless time in prayer for it. All was waste of my energy when I should have been seeking the kingdom of God and His desires for me. But I developed a strong prayer life with God through trial and error of my life.

I get almost sick when I waste time praying for unnecessary things that are not mine. I'm gonna tell you how I got delivered from this madness of empty prayer or missing the mark. I won't call it empty prayer because even in the times of me missing the mark God showed up and meet with me, we had fellowship one with another, and it was always wonderful. I was praying according to scripture Luke 18:1–8, "And he spake a parable unto them to this end, that men ought always to pray and not to faint; Saying, there was in a city a judge, which feared not God, neither regarded man: And there was a widow in that city: and she came unto him, saying, avenge me of mine adversary. And he would not for a while: but afterward he said within himself, though I fear not God, nor regard man; Yet because this widow troubleth me, I will avenge her, lest by her continual coming she weary me. And the Lord said, hear what the unjust judge saith, And shall not God avenge his own elect, which cry day and night unto him, though he bear long with them? I tell you that he will avenge them speedily. Nevertheless, when the son of man cometh, shall he find faith on the earth?"

I am like the widow woman. I will ask until God answers yes or no. I've been told no a few times too, many times actually or to wait, not now. I will take no over not now any day because God began to work patience in me during these times, and well, 40 percent of the time now, I don't get upset like I did in my younger years. When I was younger and immature, I hated when He said, "No, now, later," but I never knew when, so I got upset and stopped praying for that things and found something else to pray for, not understanding that I was delaying my prayers even more by being disobedient to God.

How I Got Delivered from Praying for Things That Wasn't Mine

It's this man of God, the preacher I listen to from time to time, not sure how I got connected to him, but it was the work of the Holy Spirit. His name is Ron Carpenter, pastor of Redemption Church in Greenville. But I heard one of his teachings—he teaches in series, I like that. So he began to talk about prayer and asking God for stuff and spending hours and hours in prayer daily for an answer from the Lord. So one day, he was concerning purchasing a piece of property for the advancement of the church. But in his times of prayer and seeking God for a yes or no, he becomes very irritated and impatient and uptight at times, which he tells his story, and his wife catches the brunt of it all plus the church.

So this one time, he was shut away in prayer, and the wife had plans for them, and she walks in and says to him, "Ron, just ask God is the property yours and get up and let's go." He said something clicked inside him like a bomb. He said she's right, so he said, "God, I'm asking you right now, is this property mine yes or no? So I don't waste any more time praying for something that belongs to someone else." And the Lord immediately asked him, "No, Ron, the property isn't yours. I have another property for you." And he said that cut out a lot of time asking, begging, pleading with God. Now he enjoys his times of fellowship with the Lord because if he wants something or desires something, he simply asks God is this mine, from property to houses to members of his church. When I heard this in 2016, it freed up a lot of my time in prayer, but sometimes, I forget to ask God is it mine or not. But not too much time goes by, and if it does, I enjoy the fellowship with my father anyway.

Step 4: Thanksgiving—prayer of thanksgiving is a prayer that expresses thanks to God. A prayer of gratitude. The Bible says in everything gives thanks. Give God thanks for your life, your limbs, health, strength, family, job for Jesus. Even if you don't have good health, you're still alive and have one more day to get it right with Him. Even if you don't have a job, believe He will provide for you anyway even if you disconnected from your family. Thank that your mother gave birth to you instead of aborting you. Thank Him that you have twenty-four-hour access to Him daily whether you use it or not.

Step 5: Request—prayer of request is an act of asking politely or formally for something. Prayers of request are you just simply talk to God in a casual sense about your wants. They are not needs but the wants. So you politely request and ask the Father like you do your earthly father with your puppy eyes can he give you what you want. You butter up to the Father, love Him more because you should already love Him, honor Him, adore Him, and spend time with Him at this point in your relationship. You should already be comfortable in knowing Him that you can cuddle up to Him on His lap and ask for you a special gift.

I imagine myself sitting on my father's lap laying on his chest asking him in a soft voice can I please have such and such. I did this with my earthly father, and it worked 98 percent of the time. So I do it with my heavenly Father too, and he answers me. He spoils me too. I'm his little girl, daddy's little girl. He showers me with stuff and blessings because I am truly the apple of my father's eye and his little girl. Nothing like a father's love for his children especially his daughters. Now I know he loves his sons too, a lot, but this is my story I'm talking about how my heavenly Father loves me and adores me, and I love and adore Him.

Agreement prayer—prayer of agreement is when you and someone else come into agreement, oneness, concerning a subject in prayer.

Matthew 18:19 (KJV) says, "Again I say unto you, that if two of you agree on earth about anything that they may ask, it shall be done for them by the father who is in heaven." I am a firm believer that some prayers will not be answered until you have someone touch and agree and join you in prayer. I really believe God set it up this way for us to avoid pitfalls of pride and selfishness. Being alone, a one-man show I call it. To say you did it alone. God knew this human side of us, so in His wisdom, He developed a system of prayer that would eliminate our pride and help us become overcomers in every area. I have to bring up pride again because I was at one time prideful in my prayers that God answered me and quickly, and I knew that God would back me up because I had performed all the rituals of Christianity, followed all the scriptures to enter into is His presence, and knew how to pray according to His will through His word to Him that He could not deny me my prayers.

People, we have wicked, evil hearts, and many don't know it until you are faced with God in prayer. Most of the time, the Holy Spirit deals with you before God can, even Jesus because of our state of mind and heart concerning the things of God. But that is a whole other subject and set of issues. My point is you need somebody, not just anybody to help you pray. I have experienced good and bad prayer partners that is why I am telling you don't get anybody, ask God to send you the right person to pray and agree with you. They must have the mind and heart of God and walk in humility and truth, or the relationship will be one-sided, and that's not agreement.

After years of a couple wrong partners, I went back to praying alone because it was safer for me and my lifestyle. I don't have time to be entangled with foolishness and mess, and that's what happened when I was the only one praying. I had a life experienced that rocked my world and called my prayer partner, and she did absolutely nothing. I mean, I didn't try to pray for peace for me.

This was day after day I called and cried until the hurt hit my heart that she didn't care about my situation or me because all her prayers had been answered through my laid down life. And at that moment, I withdrew myself from the prayer of agreement with others. I was fighting for my life and had no one to help me fight or cover me. This was a real wake-up call concerning prayer, so I did what I do best. I went on a fast and sought after God wholeheartedly. I did a shut-in at work for three weeks and called on the Lord to bring me out. See, people, I am trying to help you avoid a lot of future hurts from church people and show you how we are fickle at best. People change like the weather and don't realize it. We are selfish at best and want our way all the time. Was I upset? Yes. Was I hurt? Yes. But after I sought God, the Holy Spirit began to show me the error of my ways as well and the assignment on my life concerning prayer and whom could cover me in prayer and whom I was called to cover and protect through prayer.

So I forgave her, but I don't pray with them anymore, no love lost, I'm just at a different place in my walk with God, wiser, and I am no longer around or in contact with them. See, as you go deeper in God, people will remove themselves from your life because they don't want to give up their lives like you or sacrifice the passing pleasures of life to gain Christ. Many do, but they are few and far between. I know because I was one of them. I loved what I was doing when God snatched me, and I was good at it too. Thank God for Jesus that He came and got me, and He came to get you too. So after two years of praying alone for private matters and being an intercessor for two different pastors and one church, God sent me another prayer partner to touch and agreement on matters of my heart.

My God Sent an Agreement Prayer Partner

God has so graced me with the most humble, sweet, meek, kind, loving, understanding, upfront, real in your face prayer partner that don't mind telling you the truth about yourself in love or what thus say the Lord to you. This mighty man of God name is Minister Matthew Gibson of Joshua Media Ministries International (JMMI) staff. God connected us through JMMI in October 2016 and February 2017. Apostle Taylor personally assigned him to cover me in prayer and be my prayer partner. He has been great. They are wonderful people. When I tell you that a person can know all your past, present, and future and not judge you but love you in spite of this is what I have experience with Matthew. I call him Matthew now because after nineteen months of praying and talking, I consider him a friend of mine. That's funny because my normal self always ask people a lot of questions before I trust them or talk in detail with them. But with Matthew, the Holy Spirit took control of me.

I never got the opportunity or the desire to ask anything concerning him until almost two years later, in fact, four weeks ago as I write this book, I again asked him about himself and his heart's desires and personal life, and God had to come to me in a dream for me to get the revelation of this man. When I awake, I was different and felt different concerning Matthew and what he meant to me and had been sent to me from God. I am still unfolding parts of this revelation today, June 28, 2018, as I write this book. But I thanked him daily even more and shared with him what he has meant to me these last nineteen months.

I really don't think he has grasps the revelation of how much I needed him when God sent him because I share everything with him, and he remains calm, no excitement at all, and I questioned that as well. And he explained to me that he has been to heaven. So when you go to heaven and come back, you see things differently. You act differently. You respond differently to things. He explains that he's quiet by nature, inherited from his father, and he has passions and is very passionate about Christ and kingdom, his assignment in the kingdom, marriage, relationship, and life.

I responded like okay because I didn't know if you were crazy or dangerous. We laughed because we have a similar background in our past, but he became my friend that day, but he as always called me his buddy from day one. So I told you that to ask God to sent you the right prayer partner that you might grow in grace through love and answered prayer and avoid being hurt and vexed by the wrong people. This method will help you avoid many hurts from the saints of God, avoid many backstabbers, gossip sessions, and betrayal because of ignorance and lack of knowledge and truth. So be smart and wise. Seek the Father and ask Him to send you your assigned prayer of agreement partner. Do prayer partners change absolutely, but if God's desire that we have agreement prayers and intercessors assigned to our lives in order for us to stand for Him, He set it up that way. Use every plan devised for your success in God.

Intercessory prayer—the act of praying to a deity on the behalf of others.

In 1 Timothy 2:1–2 (KJV), which says, "I urge, then, first of all, that petitions, prayers, intercession and thanksgiving be made for all people—for kings and all those in authority, that we may live peaceful and quiet lives in all Godliness and holiness."

If the body of Christ, all believers, all church folks would just get a deep revelation of this one scripture, the world would change immediately because we would dethrone all the prince demons, principalities, prince of darkness, king demons, and warlocks because of the power of prayer and intercession. Intercession is not just a light prayer; it is a deep groaning that cannot be uttered. You have to come at your spirit with intercession prayers because you need to bypass your mind, your will, and your emotion to get to the place of God, which is the holy of holies—the inner chamber of the sanctuary; a place regarded as the most sacred or special (*Webster*).

You got to get to the holy place of God to intercede for His people because you are to only pray God's will for them, not yours. This is why people pray, and nothing happens in the other's life, and their situation and circumstances stay the same because we pray our will for people's lives, not God's. Please do a search and study on the art of prayer. It will change you, change your family and your church, and change your community. If just you get this revelation, you alone will effect change. I know because it is happening in my life from the moment God opened my eyes to this revelation. I began to effect change in many areas of my life and in the lives of others. You're reading my proof now. This was birthed through prayer, proper prayer. You're not gonna go before God any kind of way and think He will hear you, not so, not happening. Learn His way and get results.

Corporate Prayer—is described as the praying together with other people in small groups or in large groups of bodies of people. It is an important part of the church, and in Acts 2:42 (KJV), it says, "They devoted themselves to the apostles' teaching and to the fellowship. To breaking of bread and prayer." We learn that in the early church, they prayed together. Many churches need to get revelation on this scripture, and the church unity and function will change rapidly beginning with them.

Benefits of Corporate Prayer

Encouragement—praying with others can bring encouragement to members of the group. There may be those in a group who are struggling with trials and temptations. As they are not held in prayer, the Holy Spirit brings them encouragement and reassurance of God's promises.

Unity—corporate prayer knit people together in a bond of fellowship and praise. People are edified and unified in common faith. As people pray together, they build love and concern for others and display their dependence on God.

Worship—corporate prayer brings intimate communion with the savior.

Repentance—as people pray, the Holy Spirit brings conviction and draws His children to repentance.

These are some of the many experiences I have had with prayer and still learning daily to pray in my purest form of worship to God. So every day, I strive to seek Him more and humble myself in the process. I hope this will increase your love and life of prayer.

$\mathcal{C}$hapter 5

Fasting

Matthew 6:16–18 (KJV) says, "Moreover when ye fast, be not as the hypocrites, of a sad countenance: for they disfigure their faces, that they may appear unto men to fast. Verily I say unto you, they have their reward. But thou, when thou fastest, anoint thine head, and wash thy face; that thou appear not unto men to fast, but unto thy father which is in secret; and thy father which seeth in secret, shall reward thee openly."

Fasting is another requirement to a successful prayer life. You ask why? Well, in order to be confident and bold in prayer, one must fast. I really believe that if you don't fast, you will not be humbled enough to even pray. What is fasting? I'm glad you asked me.

Fasting—a fast, fasting—to abstain from all or some kinds of food or drink, especially as a religious observance (*Webster*).

Fast—to abstain from all food. To cause to abstain entirely from or limit food. A day or period of fasting (Dictionary).

Fasting or fast—a voluntary abstinence from food. Not eating. To fast. To abstain from eating. To go without food (Vine Greek New Testament Dictionary).

Fasting—a voluntary abstinence from food (Vine Greek New Testament Dictionary).

Luke 2:37 (KJV) says, "And she was a widow of about fourscore and four years, which departed not from the temple, but served God with fastings and prayers night and day."

Acts 14:23 (KJV) says, "And when they had ordained them elders in the church, and had prayed with fasting, they commended them to the Lord, on whom they believed."

Fasting Required to Cast Out Demons

Fasting had become a common practice among Jews and was continued among Christians. Matthew 17:21 (KJV) says, "Howbeit this kind goeth not out but by prayer and fasting."

In Mark 9:29 (KJV), which says, "And he said to them, this kind can come forth by nothing, but by prayer and fasting."

Fast refers to "day of atonement." Fasting required to afflict your soul.

The day of atonement was that time of the year would be one of dangerous sailing, of involuntary abstinence (perhaps, voluntary is included).

Leviticus 16:29 (KJV) says, "And this shall be a statue forever unto you: that in the seventh month, on the tenth day of the month, ye shall afflict your souls, and do no work at all, whether it be one of your own country, or a stranger that sojourneth among you."

Second Corinthians 6:5 (KJV) says, "In stripes, in imprisonments, in turmults, in labours, in watchings, in fastings."

Second Corinthians 11:27 (KJV) says, "In weariness and painfulness, in watching often, in hunger and thirst, in fastings often, in cold and nakedness."

Fasting to abstain from all or some kinds of foods and drink

Daniel's fast—to abstain from some kinds of foods.

Daniel 1:12 (KJV) says, "Prove thy servants, I beseech thee, ten days; and let them give us pulse to eat, and water to drink."

Daniel 10:2–3 (KJV) says, "In those days I Daniel was mourning three full weeks. I ate no pleasant bread, neither came flesh nor wine in my mouth, neither did I anoint myself at all, till three whole weeks were fulfilled."

As you see, there are many forms and purposes to fast as a Christian. There are certain times to fast. There are certain amount of days to fast. Certain months and dates to fast for a specific purpose or assignment. I have completed several different fast for many reasons.

At age twenty in 1996, while I was attending college, I got introduced to fasting by a woman I meet. We begin to talk about the goodness of the Lord, and she like I was a single mother. We both had relocated to Mississippi from up north. We entered into an agreement of fasting and prayer for our husbands to be joined to us that was from the Lord. We both agreed that we made poor choices with our children's fathers, but God had mercy on us. We agreed to fast three days out of seven. Monday, Wednesday, and Fridays until we received our husbands. Well, during the days of our fasting at lunchtime, we would go to the library to search the scriptures and research the Bible for the promises of God.

I would have to say God begin to move on our behalf rather quickly. Within months, I had a man surrounded me that I could not get rid of. Oh yes, they would come out the woodwork of all sorts, sizes, shapes, and cultures.

I told her, "Girl, we got to be more prespecific with our prayers to narrow down our search and wait time."

See, people, I'll be the first to confess that I did more look for him than waiting for him. The reason I was looking was because I wasn't told that the man had to find me. I thought I was to actively help God find me a husband. Now I wanted him to come from the Lord, but I wanted to choose my own husband. And the Lord sent this man who was a virgin at age twenty-six or twenty-seven if I remember correctly. Now allow me to tell you how jacked up in my mind I was and bound in unbelief, arrogance, and all the above, stupidly as well.

When this guy began to talk to me and tell me he wanted to date me, take me out, marry me, he didn't care that I had three children already. He was in love with me and thought I was the prettiest, nicest woman he ever saw and meet. Now this guy was my aunt's best friend's grandson, devout Christian, hard worker.

He said, "Oh, I have money to purchase us a brand-new home. I'm just waiting to get married to buy our home. I still live at home with my parents and save my money. I work for my father's company. I'm part owner of our business."

I said, "Okay, that's great, but I have three children and not a virgin."

He said, "I don't care. You're a good woman, mother, and loves the Lord."

This man came every other day for seven to eight months to my house y'all. I am not lying. I rejected him because he was a virgin, and I didn't want to have to teach and train a man how to have sex. I was bound by my past, living in fear of my past.

So I told him, "I'm sorry I can't marry you, but you should seek a virgin wife."

He continued to come week after week. He would just watch me interact with my children, begging to give us a great life of love, freedom, peace, and prosperity. He said, "You will never have to work another in your life if you marry me."

I still rejected this man of God because he wasn't the kind of husband I thought I deserved or that God would give to me. I thought I was supposed to get a husband with a horrible past so I could help him and become more stressed out. See, we pray and fast and ask God for many things, and when he sends them, they don't come in a way or form in which we are used to, we reject them—the blessing and God all at the same time because we lack knowledge of God and His ways.

It's like the scripture says in Luke 11:11 (KJV): "If a son shall ask bread of any of you that is a father, will he give him a stone? Or if he ask a fish, will he for a fish give him a serpent?" We ask God for His best for us, but we refuse to renew our minds and change our lives to receive His best for us. This mistake and decision caused me deadly consequences spiritually and naturally. I married a man that almost killed me several time and was very abusive and harsh to me, as you read in *The Real Antonette Come Forth* book series.

I am forty-two years old now, divorced and single. I haven't been in a relationship of any sort for almost three years. I have had many heartbreaks, disappointments, setbacks, and delays in the love and relationship department. I still seek God daily for my godly husband. The Lord had confirmed many times that He has a mate that I was created for. I know many things about this future husband and the call of God on his life, but what I do not know is whom he is yet. But it has been twenty-two years since this mistake happened on my behalf, and I know now to wait on the Lord to send my husband and to not look for him. I am not as tempted to look for him as I was twenty-two years ago, now I just got delivered from that mentality and mind-set toward men, marriage, and relationship.

During this three year of singleness, I have learned to be a wife, a helpmeet, a supporter, and the role I play to my husband. I have learned so many roles I play as a woman and not to combine nor confuse any of them. The mother, grandmother, wife, sister, daughter, aunt, counselor, teacher, mentor, friend, lover, supporter, encourager, the woman of God, etc. You have to be taught and trained to be the woman called and created you to be. You have to be willing to be corrected, lead and guided into the real you. To learn submission, real submission to your husband. To respect him with real wholehearted respect. To honor him, truly honor the man God created you for and presented you as a gift to him.

See, God is the one that gives you as a gift to the man, His king, His son. So the man has the responsibility to stay before God to create his wife that came out of his side. So I have been made for this one man of God. I have been through much training, killings of the flesh and mind-sets, cutting off people and relationships, habits, ideas, behaviors to be the wife, helpmeet I'm supposed to be. But you will read about all those changes in book five of this sequel titled *Made for Him* (God uniquely made me for my husband). Yes, I am everything he wanted in his wife and more if you asked me.

Since this my book I will say I am more than he dreamed of or imagined I would be. I'm not being arrogant or boastful or prideful, but I'm telling you whomever this man, my future husband, may be is the most favored man walking this planet because number one, I love our Lord with all my heart. I am open and honest with no secrets. He was one of the reasons I told my life testimony through my book series. I didn't want the devil to have anything He could bring up from my past to affect my future with my husband. I am a very wise woman who seeks the truth, knowledge, and direction concerning our lives in many forms. I am beautiful inside and outside. I am very easy on the eyes, and when God formed me, He formed me with beautiful curves. He formed beautiful skin, lips, hips, legs, butt, and breast. I'm really beautiful and formed and shaped exactly like my husband desired me to be. I truly am his glorious church.

As said in Ephesians 5:27–28 (KJV), "That he might present it to himself a glorious church, not having spot, or wrinkle, or any such thing; but that it should be holy and without blemish. So ought men to love their wives as their own bodies. He that loveth his wife loveth himself." This is the husband I so desire, and I know I will have. He will love me because he loves himself. He will teach me, lead me, guide me, and care for me like Christ the church and give himself for me. He had to give himself to Christ first that I may be formed and shaped to be given to him that another truth about marriage and unity, commitment. So be willing to fast and pray to give about change in yourself first and change in your life, your mind that you don't reject the work of God in your life, nor reject those he sends into your life.

Fasting open your eyes to see in the spirit and not the natural. Although it reveals and exposes all your fleshly desires, wants, and mishaps, mistakes that you may correct them. That you may learn and change for the glory of God to be revealed in you through you in your life. You cannot and will not successfully complete the will of God for your life without living a life of fasting and prayer. It is impossible to carry out such a heavy responsibility that's spiritual in the flesh.

This has been my experience on fasting. I used this example because this is the subject I'm dealing with at this point in time. Fasting and prayer to be joined to my kingly husband, have a kingdom marriage and fulfill our kingdom assignment together. I am marrying for a purpose not pleasure.

Chapter 6

Worshipper

Worshipper—a person who shows reverence and adoration for a deity. A person who feels great admiration or devotion for someone or something (*Webster*).

Worship—the feeling, expression of reverence, and adoration for a deity. Show reverence and adoration for a deity; honor with religious rites. To honor and respect someone or something as a God. To show respect and love for God or for God especially by praying, having religious services, etc. To love, to honor someone or something very much or too much (*Merriam-Webster*).

John 4:24 (KJV) says, "God is a spirit; and they that worship him must worship him in spirit and in truth."

Psalms 99:5 (KJV) says, "Exalt the Lord our God and worship at his footstool; he is holy."

Psalms 103:1–2 (KJV) says, "Bless the Lord, o my soul: and all that is within me, bless his holy name. Bless the Lord, o my soul, and forget not all his benefits."

In order to truly serve God out of a pure heart and good conscience, you must be a person of worship. I have learned that worship isn't an act of service to the Lord or to God but a lifestyle. What do I mean? I'm glad you asked. You must be one that live your day-to-day life in fellowship and consist communion with the Lord. You want your every move, decision to be toward bringing Him glory. The scripture says to in Ephesians 5:19 (KJV), "Speaking unto yourselves in psalms and hymns and spiritual songs, singing and making melody in your heart to the Lord."

Psalms 150:6 (KJV) says, "Let everything have breathe praise the Lord, praise ye the Lord."

Introduction into Praise and Worship

As a child, I always heard music. My mother played music consistently in our home, and for sure, on Sunday mornings, we heard the gospel music. My mother's side of the family were all mostly gospel singers, quartet gospel singers they were. My grandmother and her sisters began their group before I was born and the children followed suit. So I came from a singing family. Many of my family members tell me that gene skipped me, but I still sing praises aloud, and I mean aloud. That's the meaning of my middle name Lolita "to sing praises aloud."

I used to wonder why I talked louder than other women because I have a set of lungs on me. I say I have a built-in microphone. I don't need a mic; I am the mic. But I have always loved singing and music. My father played music all the time especially when he drives. He loves the blues Muddy Waters. OMG, did he love that man's music. So I was exposed to many forms of music as a child. My one aunt introduced me the down-home blues, and I fell smooth in love with them.

My older brother introduced me to pop and break dancing music. I guess y'all wondering why I'm taking you to the memory lane with my music? Because I want you to see that God has already created you in a way to worship Him through music. But we, as children, are exposed to many other forms of music including the right and wrong music. So you came here with a built-in love for music whether you like it or not, listening or not. I am one that loves music and love to sing. When I read or heard those scriptures that everything that has breath should praise the Lord I sang louder and more. And when I read the scripture to make melody in the heart to the Lord, I began to always keep a song in my heart. I always sang songs or found songs to help me through tough times. Music changes the atmosphere and changes you, your mood. This is why I always, always sing and dance.

Lord, my poor five children I used to make them slow dance with me to R&B music. I listen to a lot of R&B music to keep me in believing in love and being in love with a man, to keep my hopes up for my soul mate the man I was created for. I had a rough and harsh life most of my life, so music was an escape for me. I would sing and think about how this would be loved like this by a man because, in my reality, I was getting the opposite.

I listen to gospel music to keep my heart soft toward God and love for Jesus because they were my only hope for a peaceful life of joy and love. So I listened to gospel songs that gave me hope to fight another day, and in the process, I learned to praise the Lord for His goodness. And as I praised Him, I loved Him more, and as I loved Him more, I entered into the realm of worship. The realm of worship is where I adored Him. I loved on Him. I sat at His feet and worshipped Him. I cried out to Him. I was changed in His presence more and more each day.

Worshippers are different from praises and on different levels. This is where you see Christians at different levels. Anyone and everyone can praise the Lord because you just open your mouth and sing, clap, flip, flop, and jump like the other church folks, and they will say, "Oh, the love of the Lord."

They are praising Him. Well, yeah, they might be but only with their mouth. This is proven in Matthew 15:8 (KJV), which says, "This people draweth nigh unto me with their mouth, and honoreth me with their lips, but their heart is far from me."

See what the scripture says. This further lets me know that worship is a lifestyle not an act of service as many may think. God wants your heart. He wants you to truly worship Him in spirit and truth. It's a song I absolutely love, and it helped me with worship and music too. Its titled "The heart of Worship" by Michael W. Smith, and in his song, he sings about coming back to a heart of worship to God without any music.

He says, "When the music fades / all is stripped away / and I simply come / longing just to bring / something / that will bless your heart, / I'll bring you more than a song / for song in itself / is not what you have required. / You search much deeper within / through the way things appear / you're looking into my heart, / I'm coming back to the heart of worship, / it's all about you, / it's all about you Jesus." This is a beautiful powerful song that makes you think about the songs you sing before the Lord our God.

I also was given a teaching on "The Truth behind Hip-Hop Music" by Pastor Craig G. Lewis, a preacher out of Texas I was given DVD teachings in 2009. This changed the music I bought in my house and allowed my children to listen to. Watch the music you listen to and the singer's lifestyle. Demons are passed through music and singing. Words are being released through songs because you open your mouth. Check it out. It will change your life. I know it changed mine. And I'm striving each day to enter into the straight and narrow gate. I go to extreme measures to help narrow my way. See, I also learned we have a responsibility to cut a lot of junk and baggage out our own lives. God has already prepared the way of escape for us. We have to do our part and rid our lives of distractions to become true worshippers in lifestyle and our hearts to our king.

That's my experience on worshipping and learning more as the days go by.

$\mathscr{C}$hapter 7

Obedience

Now the word *obedience* is almost a foreign concept in the twenty-first century, especially to the youth of this day, but the older generations are just rebels to put it lightly or in layman terms. To obey anyone is almost nonexistent, even on the job, at school, in the home, and in society. People are just going about their day doing as they please, but I am not shocked at all because the holy scriptures are being fulfilled.

In 2 Timothy 3:2 (KJV), it says, "For men shall be lovers of their own selves, covetous, boasters, proud, blasphemers, disobedient to parents, unthankful, unholy."

See, when you read the scriptures, they are meant for your learning, teaching, and training and to be applied to your daily life. The issue is people read the Bible and think it was just for the apostles and people of old. That's not true. It you don't begin to read this Bible for your own self, your own life, and apply these scriptures to your daily life, in hell you will lift up your eyes. Okay, I can hear some of you readers saying she has no business saying that. That's not true. Well, allow me to give your scriptures to prove my point. Y'all should know me by now that I will do your research for you because I want you to succeed in this life for Christ. Amen.

In 2 Timothy 3:16 (KJV), it says, "All scriptures is given by inspiration of God and is profitable for doctrine, for reproof, for correction, for instruction in righteousness."

Do you understand now that these scriptures are to guide you into a life of obedience unto Christ? Listen, obedience does not come easily to us, and it's not our fault. Let me give you two foundation scripture before I began to talk more about this topic in detailed.

Psalms 51:1–6 (KJV), which says, "Have mercy upon me, O God, according to thy lovingkindness: according unto the multitude of thy tender mercies blot out my transgressions. Wash me thoroughly from mine iniquity, and cleanse me from my sin. For I knowledge my transgressions: and my sin is ever before me. Against thee, thee only, have I sinned, and done this evil in thy sight: that toud mightest be justified when thou speakest, and be clear when thou judgest. Behold, I was shapen in iniquity; and in sin did my mother conceive me."

See, in this scripture, David is telling God, "Have mercy on me because I was conceived in sin and shapen in iniquity." Allow me to explain what he saying. After the fall of Adam and Eve in the Garden of Eden. I will assume all of you know the story of Adam and Eve. If you don't, we need to really get you saved and delivered from Satan's power. But the story can be found in Genesis the first book of the Bible, the King James Version only. Many saints of old lost their lives to get us this version of the Bible over 40 authors, 66 books, and 1,189 chapters. But back to the story of obedience, I am still talking about obedience, people. After the fall of Adam and Eve, a curse hit all mankind. Everyone born was born in a fallen state of sin. Sin is and will always be trapped by our members, our body. So we were born into sin, a fallen state from the glory of God. Then shapen into iniquity. Let me backtrack for a moment and define these words for you.

Sin—is to miss the mark, a serious shortcoming (*Webster*).

Transgression—presumptuous sin, to choose to intentionally disobey, willful trespassing. Failure to do your duty.

Iniquity—is wickedness, gross injustice. A wicked act or thing. Corruption, debauchery, immorality, or depravity.

Abomination—is a thing that cause disgust or hatred. Obscenity, monstrosity.

Shapen—to be born in iniquity or that he was a sinner when he was born or that his sin could be traced back to his very birth—as one might say that he was born with a love of music or with a love for nature or with a sanguine, a phlegmatic or a melancholy temperament.

You see, there are different levels of disobedience in the eyes of God. Many people think of it's just a sin. But all is not a sin, and not all is forgiven by God. First, God has to choose to grant you forgiveness and mercy. But that's a whole other subject in itself. Don't have time to write about it, but you should study the scriptures.

So when we operate in disobedience, it's not all sin because sin is to miss the mark. But if I intentionally choose not to do what God has asked of me, now it's a transgression because I choose not to obey what I was told. When I cross the line from transgression now, I'm in iniquity. I am operating in pure wickedness because my heart is hardened because I have chosen to transgress and not obey. Oh yes, people of God, it's deep and serious. See, it may appear to be simple and just on the surface, but it runs much deeper than that. After you cross over into iniquity, your next phrase is an abomination. I think this is the worst of the worst in the sight of God because he says an abomination is anything that is beyond sin missing the mark, stronger than transgressions you willfully trespassing and pass your iniquity forms of wickedness and corruptions.

Abomination is pure disgust, hatred, obscenity, and monstrosity to God. And while I'm giving you the different forms of disobedience, I'm gonna address this issue that has taken over our country and let you see how God views it.

Homosexuality—is not a sin or a transgression nor an iniquity. Homosexuality is an abomination of desolation. (Read Genesis 19). The story of Sodom and Gomorrah destroyed. The men tried to have sex with the angels that came to destroy the city. Genesis 19:13 (KJV) says, "Because we are going to destroy this place. The outcry to the Lord against its people is so great that he has sent us to destroy it."

Homosexuality is unnatural. It's not normal to be attracted to the same sex. People are not born homosexuals. They are taught to be homosexuals. It is a strong demon, the spirit that takes hold of people, groups of them and take over.

Adultery is a sin and or transgression—it's not right, but it is a natural course of the man and woman. You choose to cheat on your spouse, no one makes you. I say sin first because you missed the mark of being faithful and fell short. Say transgression because you may have intentionally chosen to have sex with someone other than your spouse. But it's not an abomination to God like homosexuality. You see the difference. God is and you should be disgusted with homosexuality, it's unnatural, disgust, obscenity, and a monstrosity in the nostrils of God. He has a deep hatred for it because you cannot reproduce children being this way. Homosexuality stops the production of babies being born. Don't you understand that? It is anti-God. Anything that is used to prevent kingdom builders, world changers, and giant slayers from being birthed and produced to advance the kingdom of God is an abomination of desolation. Abortion, let's talk about that too, another abomination of desolation. You killing children to satisfy your own selfish desires and not wanting to be a parent to birth kings into this world. Satan has a hold on you too.

But all this obedience, sin, iniquity, transgressions, and abominations in this twenty-first century, there is a way of escape, a way out, a way of deliverance out of it all, and it is through Jesus the Christ—His life, His way, His truth. Read this next scripture. It's going to bless your socks off your feet and your weave out your head.

Hebrews 5:7–10 (KJV) says, "Who in the days of his flesh, when he had offered up prayers and supplications with strong crying and tears unto him that was able to save him from death, and was heard in that he feared; though he were a son, yet learned he obedience by the things which he suffered; and being made perfect, he became the author of eternal salvation unto all them obey him; called of God a high priest after the order of melchisedec."

See, people of God, even our Lord Jesus had to learn obedience because He too was born into sin and shapen into iniquity because he was born into the flesh. Suffering produces obedience. Let me prove my point. When your mother or father tell you, "Little Johnny, don't run in the driveway. You will fall and hurt yourself." You being born into sin has a built-in system called sin that says I can run and not fall. The first day you succeed you think to yourself, "I told you I would not fall. My parents don't know what they are talking about."

Day two, "Johnny don't run in the driveway."

Well, Johnny ran because he got away with it yesterday, but today, Johnny falls in the driveway after running five miles per hour. He falls and tumbles. Now Johnny has a broken waist because he tried to break his fall. A busted forehead because when his waist broke, he continued to tumble. Both knees and shoulder have concrete burns and bruises. So Mom runs outside.

"Oh, Johnny, I told you not to run in the driveway." Blood everywhere she calls the EMT. They come to pick up Johnny. Johnny has emergency surgery for his waist. CT scan for his head, and x-rays for shoulder and legs. He is hospitalized for three days because he is only six years old. After three months, Johnny has fully recovered, and he is back playing outside in the driveway.

Mom says again for the ten-thousandth time, "Johnny, don't run in the driveway. You will fall and hurt yourself."

This time, Johnny says, "Yes, ma'am, Mom, I promise not to run."

Not only did Johnny obey but not running. Johnny never left out the garage playing. He never played in the driveway again. Now Johnny is thirty, telling his son, "Hey, Johnny Jr, don't run in the driveway. You will fall and hurt yourself."

Johnny learned obedience from the things he suffered, a broken waist, bruised head, and body. Now he is teaching from experience because he has learned to obey through suffering, and you always remember that the sufferings you go through when you survive them, you come out with something you didn't have going in. Don't refuse obedience. Disobedience is more than a sin; it's more than transgression or iniquity. It can lead to abomination. Don't tempt the Lord thy God to destroy you or the fruit of your womb.

This is my take on obedience.

C hapter 8

Tither/Giver-Sower

Now, this is the chapter that many of you wished I would have skipped over. That is if you are a person of greed, a person of selfish intentions and desires. A person full of pride, self-will, stubbornness, hard-heartedness. See, I have to recap from the previous chapters because they all go hand in hand. People, I am telling you that all these are connected to each other, and it's almost impossible to have one without the other. If you do, then hip, hip hooray for you. But I'm telling you, one lead to the other for me. Some may have come in different order, but to the best of my ability, this is how it unfolded for me. Granted I was taught some things as a child, and it was a learned behavior I was taught such as this chapter.

I was taught by my father to automatically be a giver, especially of the finances. Now I know most of your hairs are standing up on your head, neck, and arms. But I tell you the God's honest truth. My father taught all of us that was around him to give of your finances first and foremost. If you can be present with someone, send your love through money, through gifts. I was late in life baby for my father for he was fifty-two when I was born by my mother. I was their only child together. He had grown children older than my mom, and Mom had three other children older than me. So because they weren't living together, my father would come to visit me a lot and pick me up for the weekends, summers, school breaks but very active in my life.

When he came to visit me, he always bought me a gift of some sort more than one or took me shopping each weekend for all my life with him. My father gave me gifts until he left me, and I was grown with children, but he still called me baby, his baby, and treated me as such. So much so I was pregnant with my babies and still lay on my father's chest and sat in his lap. You got to remember I birthed my first child at age thirteen. But that's in the series if you haven't read it. He would bring groceries to our house each week. He would deliver groceries to many houses in many towns and cities. He would pay peoples rent, light bills, gas bills, purchase clothes for their children. He was just a generous man. Truly from the heart, he would give you his last and did many times, but because he was a natural giver, he never lacked. He could start a business out of nothing and did it time and time again from car lots to grocery stores, tire shops, fruit stands, houses, clothes, hair products.

I think my father owned almost every kind of business except a restaurant to my remembrance, but remember, he was here fifty-two years before I got here. These are all the businesses I've seen starting in my twenty-one years of being with him. But the amazing thing about my father wasn't that he was a huge giver and businessman, but he operated in a supernatural grace to perform all these tasks and acts of service. My father was illiterate—unable to read or write. That's right. He could not read one word, I mean, not one. He could barely write his name. When I was about ten or eleven, I found out that my father could not read or write, but each morning, he could get the newspaper and look in it at the breakfast table. I mean every morning as I was a child.

When I would bring books to him to read to me, he would say, I need glasses and tell me to pick the hairs out his chin. So I would lay across his chest in the bed and pick the hairs as he talked to me, and he went to sleep most of the time. But that was a special time for us. He would tell me the stories of me laying on his chest like a baby playing in his face. And how special I was to him, and I meant the world to him. See, people, my father had the grace to make you feel special in his presence. I don't care if you were a boy, girl, man, or woman, drunk, drug addict, pimp, prostitute, thief, whatever he treated you with respect and won't judge you.

If you had a drug problem or issues, my father hated to see people beg for drugs, drinks, or whatever he would give it to the people, person. Yes, he sold drugs, many of them, but he had a heart for people. So people say to me all the time, "Antonette, I don't see how you do everything you do. Start multiple companies without a business loan, no partners, no investors, no staff, and no degrees, skills, or training."

That's correct. You read it correctly. No degrees, no skills or no training, and no technology knowledge at all. I can operate in the realm of entrepreneurship because I inherited my father's genes, his DNA, and I was taught by him. I studied his behavior, his way of life, his mannerism, how he dealt with people, how he treated people, how he loved his family, his children, his grandchildren, how he honored his mother and father. His father passed before I was thought of, but he spoke highly of his father because he raised him. Even though his mother gave him away to his father, my father honored his mother and took care of her until he left. If you follow a person closely and learn from them, honor them what they operate in will fall on you.

Let me show you how my father and I are alike. He could not read and write. I struggle to this day with reading and writing. I barely passed my GED test. The only college degree I have is a CNA license, certified nursing assistant license, and that only took six weeks to achieve. I jumped up and down when I passed my state test, but it was basic hands-on skills. I am excellent at acts of service. I can service you in excellence as I do always. I cannot work a computer or type. The Holy Spirit downloaded just enough grace into me to achieve the assignments God has for me. The Lord gave me all my business plans in dreams and visions, and I wrote them out with a pen and spiral notebook. *The Real Antonette Come Forth* book series and even this book here was all typed with two fingers. I cannot type, people. I am telling you the God heaven's truth. I, Antonette Smith, forty-two-year-old woman, CEO of Jentle Touch in Home Care, CEO of Real Antonette Come Forth, CEO of Mz.

Nette's Glory (braiding salon), founder of Empowerment Ministry, evangelistic teacher of the gospel of Jesus Christ, teacher, life coach, mentor, speaker, seminar instructor, philanthropist, full-time online college student obtaining my early childhood development license.

Today's date is August 27, 2018, Monday. I cannot type or work a computer and have no previous training, schooling nothing to do all I am doing today. All these gifts and talents were given to me by my fathers, my earthly father and my heavenly father. I have taken two courses for keyboarding it will not stick with me. I don't even know the home row keys still to this day. People, I am telling you I have written them out, practice them, slept on them, prayed to learn, and remember them, and nothing has happened. I've been trying to learn to type since I was sixteen years old.

People, I am telling you this is the grace of God at work in me. All my life I have prayed and asked God to keep me in a place of humility where I would always need the Lord. And I have concluded that he was blocked my ability to learn human knowledge and wisdom to keep me from pride. See, I can't take the credit for anything, not only can I not type or barely read, but I can't speak well either. I am totally depended on my Lord. He has given me the tongue of the learned and an ear to hear what the Spirit says to communicate at the times its needed for business, ministering, teaching, and so forth. He graces me with knowledge to operate my computer for classes and writing my books, nothing else. I just learned a little for my Facebook page because that for ministry purposes only, but I don't know all the ins and outs of it, nor the other sites like Twitter, Instagram. I don't have a clue.

I can't take the credit for anything at all because it's not me doing it, it's him. I just yield myself to be used. I know you sitting there like what in the world is going on. Yes, indeed, this is the power of God at work. This is why I know God can use you and take and make something out of nothing. I stay before him in prayer and fasting to get instructions, guidance on what He wants me to do. He even dresses me. I don't choose my clothes. See, people, the Lord has me telling you all my business. Well, all his business. I never choose my clothes. My father used to choose them. Then my ex-husband used to choose them. The ones I choose, I snuck and purchased them for high school and got caught and beaten by my ex-husband. So after he left me in 2007, I was at a loss. I would only purchase clothes similar to the ones I already had until 2014 the Lord freed me with His spirit and bondage. Then the Lord began to teach me how to dress.

When I am having book signings and church events where I'm ministering, I wear whites and creams dresses or pant suits. When I host an empowerment seminar or event, I wear red. When I host luncheon or dinners, an hour of empowerment lectures for empowerment ministry, I wear black. Now I have worn a black dress to a book signing, I have to wear black for empowerment seminar, but my point is I am instructed to wear certain colors for each endeavor colors that have meaning to God and to me. Even in my businesses, I wear certain colors and only use certain colors. But he wanted me to share that with someone to let you know it's okay if someone else choices your clothes, so what. Especially women get bent out of shape because they want to wear what they want to wear instead of what their husbands prefer them to wear.

I love the Lord choosing my clothes. You know why? Because he pays for them all, all of the dresses, shoes, jewelry, and he gets me a new outfit for each event. I like to say that's part of my reward for obeying. You can call it materialistic if you want to, but God knows how I went without any new clothes so my children could have the best of the best, and I didn't mind. God knows how many children I have clothed in my lifetime. See, I am still talking about being a giver, not just in your finances, but a giver of yourself. See how I connected the two with my personal private covenant with my Lord. You must become a giver of yourself in this life. Yield you desires, your will, your wants to Jesus and lay them at His feet. Lay down your life, and He will pick it up and give you marvelous things you didn't ever imagine. Jesus gave His life that we might have a life. He laid down His will for the Father's will. We have to do the same, live a laid down life. Give of your finances.

As per Matthew 6:19–21 (KJV), it says, "Lay not up for yourselves treasures upon earth, where moth and rust doth corrupt, and where thieves break through and steal: but lay up for yourselves treasures in heaven, where neither moth nor rust both corrupt, and where thieves do not break through and steal: for where your treasure is, there will your heart be also." See, from this one scripture, I can tell you where your heart is, what you love the most. It's called a paper trail. I can look at your bank account or money and tell you exactly what and who you love the most. If you love the father and Jesus like your mouth claim you do, your bank accounts will reflect it. If you love Jesus the way you claim, then your daily life will reflect it. How you live each day shows who and what you love and care about the most.

Sower—someone who sows, farmer, granger, husbandman, sodbuster, a person who operates a farm (*Webster*). The Bible says we are sowers, and we plant seeds for harvest.

Genesis 8:22 (KJV) says, "While the earth remainth, seedtime and harvest, and cold and heat, and summer and winter, and day and night shall not cease."

In 2 Corinthians 9:10 (KJV), it says, "Now he that ministereth seed to the sower both minister bread for your food, and multiply your seed and increase the fruits of your righteousness."

I love the way Dr. Mike Murdock of the Wisdom Center Church of Haltom City, Texas, puts the art of sowing and reaping. The Bible is two parts, the person of Jesus and the principles of Jesus. The person of Jesus doesn't have anything to do with your prosperity, but the principles of Jesus as everything to do with your prosperity. Prayer don't have anything to do with your prosperity neither, but the principles decide your prosperity. This man has blessed me beyond measure, and I walk in mounts of wisdom because of Dr. Mike Murdock. I have studied his life and ministry for over eleven years now. About 55 percent of the successes in my life has come from this man mentoring me. That's right over have I know and learned and operate in I learned from Dr. Mike Murdock powerful man of wisdom. That doesn't take away from what I have learned from other men and women of God. I am telling you my process to prosperity, wealth, health, and wholeness and whom God sent for me to sit at their feet and learn and glean from them. I have learned from money to living single, to living divorced, to single parenting, to womanhood, books, knowledge, sowing, reaping, harvest, the word, and so much more from Him.

Galatians 6:7 (KJV) says, "Be not deceived; God is not mocked. For whatsoever a man soweth, that shall he also reap."

Dr. Mike Murdock teaches that you will reap what you sow. If you sow joy, you reap joy, if you sow money, you reap money, if you sow kindness, you reap kindness. He explains that you are a walking warehouse of seed. You have everything in you to create what you want. Never ever sow a seed without giving it an assignment. When I learned this principle, my life changed drastically. Because before, I use to just give away money, pay people bills, give gifts, furniture and of myself, and say God will bless me in return not the people. That wasn't true at all. I knew nothing about the principles of God nor Jesus.

This is when I learned 60 percent of Jesus ministry He taught on money, the fish even bought Him money to pay taxes here on earth. What does that tell you? Even the Lord Jesus had to operate by the principles of the Bible and obey the laws of the land. He didn't say, "Well, this earth belongs to my father. I didn't have to pay taxes." But no, He told the disciples to get the money out of the fish mouth and go pay our taxes. But the Christians today avoid paying taxes at all cost to themselves. If they don't have children to carry for a refund, they don't file at all. You know why? Their money has become their God, and they don't know the principles of sowing and reaping. So when I learned years ago, I give with purpose. I sow with purpose. I give my seed an assignment.

I also had to learn about the soil I sow into. Not all soil is good soil. Meaning, not all people are good to sow into. I wasted hundreds and thousands of dollars maybe millions by that point sowing out of ignorance. But God knew the motive of my heart, and He began to teach me the correct way to be blessed beyond measure. Its times, seasons, and reasons to sow for concern things and for certain people. I sowed my way out of poverty, out of heartbreak, out of despair, out of discontentment. I sowed into my future, my children's future, grandchildren's future, great-great-great-grandchildren's future by applying the principles of Jesus and loving the person of Jesus. Two separate operations. People of God, it's more to Jesus, more to the Bible, more to the kingdom, more to Christianity than we can fathom. I learn, see, and hear something new every single day. The scriptures are true each day with the Lord gets sweeter and sweeter.

This is a promise from the Father concerning tithes.

Tithes says in Malachi 3:7–12 (KJV):

> Even from the days of your fathers ye are gone away from mine ordinances, and have not kept them. Return unto me, and I will return unto you, saith the Lord of host. But ye said, wherein shall we return? Will a man rob God? Yet ye have robbed me, but ye say, wherein have we robbed thee? In tithes and offerings. Ye are cursed with a curse; or ye have robbed me, even this whole nation. Bring ye all the tithes into the storehouse, that there may be meat in mine house, and prove me now herewith, saith the Lord of hosts, if I will not open you the windows of heaven, and pour you out a blessing, that there shall not be room enough to receive it. And I will rebuke the devourer for your sakes, and he shall not destroy the fruits of your ground; neither shall your vine cast her fruit before the time in the field, saith the Lord of hosts."

Okay, let me break this down in English terms that you may understand what was said. I know that a lot of pastors, preachers, and ministers always use this scripture to convince you to give money to God or to the work of God, to pay your tithes because you are a Christian or a member of the church. But have you ever wondered about the people that don't have jobs or income? Are they cursed with a curse because they have no tithes or money to give to the church or work of God? See, we, as people, use the scriptures for our own personal gain or to benefit us at that time. Oh yes, we can twist and misquote, misinterpret everything God said about money just so we don't have to pay our tithes. Oh, we say I'm not taking care of any pastor and his family, he can get a job like me, work like I work. But you see, Jesus whole ministry about 60 percent of it dealt with money, currency, finances, and companies. But we skip over those scriptures because it requires us to give of our treasures, our heart. But don't you know God loves a cheerful giver? If you give with an attitude of not wanting to give, God doesn't accept it anyway. But there is hope for you, precious people. Learn from your mistakes because we all have had them. I have operated in all the below situations that's why I know it real to you and know how you think. God has to fill your heart with love for Him for you to obey Him and become a giver and a tither.

But in English terms here we go. Many organizations such as minister's alliance, freemasonry or masonry, illuminati, vice lords, gangster disciples, insurance companies, lawyer's retainer fees, country clubs, unions, medical practices, police forces, security companies all cost you a monthly fee for protection against a disaster, sudden event, accident, protection from thieves, criminals. To be a part of the clip, the social scene, the high society, the who's who clubs. In case of a lawsuit, house fire, flooding, or job loss. Protection from injustice law treatment. We pay all these companies thousands of dollar each month to provide service just in case something happens to us or to our belongings. But we don't give God one cent a month when He is the one that gave you everything you have that you trying to protect. You see how messed up in the mind we are as people? You see where our treasures are.

Oh, I got to get insurance on my house in case it burns down or floods, but it's not covered for a tornado. Oh, I got to get insurance on my car in case somebody hit me. Oh, I got to have an insurance policy in case my husband dies, I will be taken care of, And all this crap we spend our money on and almost never use it or get back what we put into the insurance premiums because soon as you drive off the lot with that 2018 BMW, the value dropped $10,000 or more. Soon as the thirty days pass your home as devalued by 2 percent to 5 percent depending on the market. We spend thousands of dollars to be members of clubs with people that don't even like you and sit and drink tea talking about your shoes and children are a mess. The thousands of dollars a year to be a part of a pastor group that can't agree one two scriptures let alone the whole Bible, and don't respect you or your wife. But see, these are things we deem important to us, and society has told you that lie by the government forcing you to get all these insurances, and we do need them by all means but not at the expense of robbing God of what is His.

Take a look at the American dollar bills, its currency, it reads "in God we trust." Even the money knows it has most people heart than God does. But we look right over those words because the God they are referring to is money, manna, moola, dineros. Another thing I want you to consider concerning money in the natural is our United States government again. It knows the power of money. That's why they take theirs off the top. Before you even see your check, the IRS has taken theirs from you because they know people are fickle at best. We say one thing and do something else. They take out social security tax 6.2 percent, state tax 7 percent, federal tax 11 percent, Medicare tax 1.45 percent. Those amounts differ according to the state you live in and its over 25 percent of your gross income, but you're not arguing with your boss or the government about taking your money.

You get up every day and go to work just so they can take your money before you see it. And, oh Lord, if you work overtime, they are taking all of that. And I say we because I'm not leaving myself out by any means like I have arrived and given God all my money, but I can promise you I give God 80 percent of my gross income. I tithe off my gross to show God it's not mine in the first place. When you tithe off your net pay, you are saying this is my money to God. Now please listen to me. These are my own deep thoughts about tithing and giving to God. I am telling you my process to prosperity, wealth, health, and wholeness. This is what has worked for me, so don't start telling people Antonette said God said tithe off your gross income.

Antonette said that's the arrangements I made with God to show Him that my money is His money, and He can use it as He pleases. And He does, and I'm blessed beyond measure. Listen, God is the best lender you can lend your money to. He always pays back triple and in more than one way. You may lend God say $125 to pay someone's water deposit. And you need a promotion on your job, and God grants it to you because you lent Him money for one of his children's needs. This is how I think, people God. I am telling you the truth. I have done this for years whether to churches, ministry, paying people bills, buying them food, clothing, gas, whatever to help someone in need because I know what matters the most to me. What matters the most to me may not matter at all to you, so you do what matters to you, but don't rob God and curse yourself in the process of living this life on earth.

God said, "Look, bring me one dollar from every ten dollars I give you. That's how much I love you to give you nine dollars, and I take one dollar, and because you love me enough to give me one dollar of your dollars, I'm so happy I'll open the windows of heaven and pour you out a blessing that you won't have room to receive."

He didn't say open a door. He said a window. Do you know the huge difference in a door and a window? Huge difference and God said you couldn't even contain the blessings from the window based on your one dollar. But then He promised to rebuke the devour for your sake. Don't you know people pay for protection from the mob, the gangs, and drug lords all are security for the protection of people. And we pay them faithfully and millions because they protect our lives, don't they? But God the Creator say give me one dollar out of ten dollars, and I will protect you from all danger, the devil, Satan's attacks on your life, the life of your children and grandchildren, protection for your home, jobs, finances, etc. All for one dollar, and we refuse to pay God to protect all concerning us because we can't see Him, or we don't know Him.

We don't love Him. We don't trust Him. When I got the revelation of this scriptures years ago in my early teens, I said I'm paying my tithes. God can protect me from everything and everybody. I'm in because I was always under attack from a child by Satan, my ex-husband, family, friends, people in general. It was always something, and I was always doing something that threatens my life and freedom. But I got a revelation that if I paid my tithes, my life would be preserved by God. I would not die before my time. I will not miss my times of appointments with Him if I obeyed. Now there were times I missed my tithes, and I was cursed, didn't work, things were hard to accomplish because I stop paying my monthly dues for protection. See, people of God, you think it's the devil, Satan, demons, people that are blocking your progress, your blessings, but it's you. You have robbed God with tithes and offerings, and the grounds know you have robbed God, so they will not produce for you. You cursed with a curse. But repent for robbing God and begin to pay your tithes the next payday. Those of God people that volunteer their services and life to ministry and don't receive income give God hours of fasting, a sacrifice of self is tithes as well.

This is my definition and explanation of giving-sowing and tithing. Don't allow the devil to trick you into believing you giving your money to a man or woman. When you pay your tithes, you're giving to God, and it is God that will reward you. I pray this chapter has blessed you to see money differently. It takes money to fund the work of God. Money moves the earth, and prayer moves heaven. Prayer will never move the earth because it's not created for the earth it's created for heaven to release to earth. Money will never move to heaven because it's not needed in heaven. Its purpose is for the earth. That's why you will never see money fall from the sky. Money doesn't come from the heavens, it comes from the earth, it comes from the trees that came from the earth. You see that revelation. That's why prayer can't work on earth; it's a heavenly operation to release the powers from heaven to come to heaven.

Let that sink into your spirit before you read the next chapter.

Chapter 9

Servant

Servant—a person who performs duties for others, especially a person employed in a house on domestic duties or as a personal attendant. A devoted helpful follower or supporter. One that serves others; a public servant; especially: one that performs duties about the person or home of a master or personal employer.

Matthew 10:24 (KJV) says, "The disciple is not above his master; nor the servant above his Lord." What Jesus is saying to us is if He had to be a servant, so do we.

Philippians 2:3–7 (KJV) says, "Let nothing be done through strife or vainglory; but in lowliness of mind let each esteem other better than themselves. Look not every man on his own things, but every man also on the things of others. Let this mind be in you, which was also in Christ Jesus: who, being in the form of God, thought it not robbery to be equal with God: but made himself of no reputation, and took upon him the form of a servant, and was made in the likeness of men."

Jesus is saying to us to put others before yourself, look to their needs first instead of your own. Be of service to people, not just in the church but in the community.

Mark 9:34–35 (KJV) says, "But they held their peace: for by the way they had disputed among themselves, who should be the greatest. And he sat down, and called the twelve, and saith unto them, if any man desire to be first, the same shall be last of all, and servant to all."

Jesus is saying to us be of help to any and all forms of people, saints and sinners alike.

Go clean the widow house, go babysit for the single mother, go take the fatherless boys for haircuts, teach the trouble teen girl how to cook and sew, clean your church's sanctuary, cut the sick neighbor's grass until he gets better, comfort the grieving mother, go give the divorced mother a break from her stresses, go to the grocery for the pregnant unwed mother whom can barely walk, go support the single father whom wife died of illness and left three children behind. It's so many ways we can be of service to people and be a servant.

That's one thing I embedded into my children, godchildren, now my grandchildren, youth group, and anyone that is around me. You must have a servant heart to be close to me. I don't allow people that don't like to serve me in my midst that much. Now I do understand people are different, and I get that, but you are the company you keep. I also understand that I can be a bit extreme to many people, it drove my ex-husband crazy. And my children are still traumatized by me making them give their beds up for a houseguest, give their clothes and toys to children in need, helping me deliver food to people house, babysitting hundreds of children during their life, cooking and feeding people from our home. They are all grown and good servants, but they say, "Mom, we love you, but no one is living with us, and our children will have their own beds and not share. And we don't mind helping people, but they got to come to get their children, and they can't stay either. We will help pay water, lights, give clothes, sheets, whatever, but you go too far with the giving, Mom."

I laugh at my babies still today when they tell me that because they have always been so supportive of me in everything I have done and still do to this day. So I purchase all my children and grandchildren their own beds and bedroom suites and help furnish their homes because they allowed many strangers to live in their homes as children all their lives until they left home and did it with a great attitude because I taught them by example and told them this is how Jesus is and wants us to be.

This is my experience of being a servant.

*C*hapter 10

Blessing

Genesis 12:1–3 (KJV) says, "Now the Lord had said unto Abram, get thee out of thy country, and from thy kindred, and from thy father's house, unto a land that I will show thee: and I will make of thee a great nation, and I will bless thee, and make thy name great; and thou shalt be a blessing: and I will bless them that bless thee, and curse him that curseth thee: and in thee shall all the families of the earth be blessed."

After you have made the Word of God your foundation for living, after you have accepted the fact that you are as a filthy rag, accepted truth about yourself, and sought the path of honesty, after facing truth of you needing help, deliverance, and guidance to live a better life to become a better you by embracing humility fully and wholeheartedly, making prayer and fasting your lifestyle and way of life daily, learning to seek the Father in spirit and truth and be the worshipper He is looking for daily, walking out this newfound life of joy, peace, training, commitment, love, teaching, learning the ways of Christ through obedience by which we suffer many things to become like Jesus our Lord to be pleasing to the Father.

Once obedience is worked into you, and you operate and live in the spirit of obedience, your acts of service, tithes, and giving become that much more easier to do to give to God's work, to help His people, being the chief servant of them all, being a servant to all you come in contact with young or old. You will never lead unless you learn to follow first. Follow the ways of Christ and walk as He walked, life as He lived, give as He gave, worship as He worshipped, pray as He prayed, fast as He fasted, remain honest through humility by searching the Word of God then and only then will God make you a blessing.

Becoming a blessing is a process. God promises if you do this, He will do that. God's promises are always predicated upon your obedience to His commands or words. God said, "Get from among your kindred, your family in other words, and go to a land I will show you." He didn't say, "If you go, I will give it to you, but I will show you the promise land. For your obedience in leaving, I will make thee a great nation."

See, people got it all wrong. They do this and do that, enter into agreements with people in hopes of becoming a great nation. When all they have to do is obey God's Word. He said, "I will make thee a great nation. I will bless thee. I will make thy name great, and thou shall be a blessing." When I got a revelation of this one scripture many years ago, I say, "Okay, Lord. I place my life in your hands. You make me into the woman you called me to be."

I was eighteen years old when I said that prayer to the Lord and He has been working in me ever since that day to make me what He called me to be. People of God, we work too hard. We work too much on the wrong stuff. Mainly out of ignorance, but nevertheless, we're wasting time trying to make ourselves great. We want to be important. We want to be accepted. We want to be viewed as the next best thing, top of the barrel, and the cream of the crop. But we do things in our own strength, and they will sometimes work in our favor. We might make it to the top, the promised land, but will you stay in that position? Whatever it took for you to get there, you must continue to do to stay there. But when God exalts you and make you great, you lay down your life, and He picks it up. It is Him doing the work, not you. See the difference.

He is the one making the deals and arranging meetings on your behalf that you become great, not you calling everyone, getting meetings. Look, the Bible is true. I had received a revelation years ago about the Bible, and people promoting themselves, and I still practice it today to a certain degree. I am loaded with many gifts and talents, titles from God own, but that isn't what I say when I meet people. I say, "Hello my name is Antonette Smith." And once you be around me long enough, you will see what gifts, talents, skills I possess. I think people that always use a title to introduce themselves suffer from false identity because we don't know who God has called us to be, and we're trying to make ourselves and name great.

See my point I am making about you promoting yourself? And then God says, "I will bless them that bless you, and curse them that curse you. People, I have witnessed this with my own eyes. I warn people that are near me, or I'm in a relationship with on any level when they began to turn from me or against me for whatever reasons, I say to them. Okay, now, you might want to change how you approach or handle me because it will not work out well for you. I'm warning you that if you don't address this or that issue, I will have to leave your life. And when I leave, you will feel it. I mean literally feel the presence of God and favor leave your life because I know He is with me. I'm not boasting or being prideful. I'm telling you the truth I have experienced this for years. And if you walk in any kind of anointing, grace, glory of God you have witnessed, God curse people that has wronged you or cursed you. He is a God of His word. This is why I could forgive all my abusers and users of my past because somehow or another, God have allowed me to witness or hear about the suffering or dying of horrible deaths or becoming deadly ill unto death. I mean sufferings.

And one time, God had to give me the scripture Proverbs 24:17 (KJV), which says, "Rejoice not when thine enemy falleth, and let not thine heart be glad when he stumbleth" because the first time he showed me one of my enemy's suffering, I was like, "Yes, Lord, make them suffer for molesting me." Oh, I was happy with joy. Even though it wasn't gonna erase what happened to me, but at least I see God is punishing them for hurting me. But years later, He corrected my attitude toward my enemies once I was at a place of contentment with Him to talk to me about this topic. God is so merciful and gracious. Even though people hurt His children, He still wants His children to have the right heart toward their friends and foes to walk in love with Him and forgiveness. But you have to embrace humility to accept this kind of correction from the Lord. I pray that me sharing my process to prosperity, wealth, health, and wholeness has given you the tools you need to complete your process or begin your process. I will give you a few more methods and things I do to help me along my way in becoming a better me in Christ.

*C*hapter 11

Bonus Chapter Become a Student of the Word Be Willing to Learn

You must have a teachable spirit to grow, progress, and succeed in the kingdom of God. It's all about learning the ways of God through the teaching of Christ. Examples from many fathers and mothers before us. Learn from their failures as well as their successes.

James 1:21 (KJV) says, "Wherefore lay apart all filthiness and superfluity of naughtiness, and receive with meekness the engrafted word, which is able to save your soul."

This scripture is saying be yielded, be humble to learn and receive instruction to save your soul, save your life.

Read men and women books, and listen to their teachings to give you hope, inspiration, and guide for living the Christian life. All ministers, pastors, teachers, apostles carry a different anointing. They are called to do a specific work for Christ in the body. Some anointing is healing, some prosperity, some faith, some holiness, some teaching of gifts. I learned this years ago from the Holy Spirit that I must get something from a variety of leaders to be perfect in my walk with God. I had to learn body life. Every joint supply a supply of the spirit of Jesus Christ. And God designed it that way so we will need each other and not to be independent. Some of these men and women of God I listen to their sermons for years, read their books, or both and still do.

I just got introduced to one two years ago. Apostle David E. Taylor has revolutionized my life completely. He has bought Jehovah down off His throne like the days of Moses. This is why I say He has revolutionized my life. The other men and women of God revolutionized my life when I gleaned from them as well. People, you will have many teachers and few fathers in the gospel because they don't want to pay the price to walk in the anointing that is needed for deliverance for a mass of people, but I learned from them all. I still walk in what I learned from them all and learning more each day.

Apostle David E. Taylor's books *Face-to-Face Appearances of Jesus: The Ultimate Intimacy*; *My Trip to Heaven: Face-to-Face with Jesus*; *Inheritance by Lineage*; and *Triumph in Humility: Victory over Pride*. Smith Wiggle Worth's *Spiritual Gifts, The Holy Spirit, The Anointing,* and *The Power of Faith*. John G. Lake's *The Flow of the Spirit: Divine Secrets of a Real Christian Life*, and *God's Generals*. Witness Lee's *Lessons on Prayer*. Andrew Murray's *The Deeper Christian Life*, and *The Ministry of Intercession*. Charles Spurgeon's *Grace and Power: Trading Our Weaknesses*. Dwight L. Moody's *The Overcoming Life*. Dr. Lester Sumrall's *Demons the Answer Book,_Demonology and Deliverance II*, and *Angels to Help You*.

William Seymour's *The Great Azusa Street Revival*. R. A. Torrey's *The Presence and Work of the Holy Spirit* and *How to Study the Bible for Greatest Profit*. R. C. Blakes Sr.'s *Tongues of Fire*. Van G. Gill's *Redemption Concluded*, and *Leviticus: A Study in Holiness*. Mike Murdock's *101 Wisdom Keys, The Bridge Called Divorce, Finances*, and *The Uncommon Leader*. Larry Huch's *10 Curses That Block the Blessing*. T. D. Jakes's *Woman Thou Art Loosed, A Satisfied Woman, He-Motions, Reposition Yourself: Living Life without Limits*, and *The Lady, Her Lover, and Her Lord*.

Dr. Cindy Trimm's *Commanding Your Morning, The 40 Day Soul Fast: Your Journey to Authentic Living*, and *Rules of Engagement: The Art of Strategic Prayer and Spiritual Warfare*. Myles Munroe's *Single, Married, Separated, and Life after Divorce; Understanding the Purpose and Power of Woman*; and *Singleness and Finding a Mate*. Juanita Bynum's *No More Sheets: The Truth about Sex, The Threshing Floor*, and *Matters of the Heart*.

Noel Jones's "Successfully Single." Leroy Phoenix's *Faith Series.* David Franklin's "Free from Sin (Romans 6)," "Hindrances in Sonship," and "Set Your Heart to Obey." Jesse Duplantis's *Heaven: Close Encounters of God Kind, Living Off the Top of the Barrel,* and "How Money Works." Dr. Bill Winston's "Stop Thinking Small God Wants You to Be Rich," "All Debts Cancelled, God Said So," and "Way unto That Mountain, Be Thou Removed."

Joyce Meyer's molestation sermons, *Approval Addiction: Overcoming Your Need to Please Everyone,* and *Battlefield of the Mind.* Mary K. Baxter's *A Divine Revelations of Hell.* Rick Joyner's *The Final Quest.* Iyanla Vanzant's *In the Meantime and Faith in the Valley.* And many, many, many more. These will be a great starting point to increase your passion and pursuit of God.

God bless you and your journey called life.

Love,
Antonette

Coming Soon

Book 2. *After The Pain: Danger of Good desires at the Wrong Time for the Wrong People*

Book 3. *My Life as a Caregiver: How I Became the Best in My Field*

Book 4. *The Heart of the Matter: God Cleansing My Insides and Me Facing Truth about Myself*

Book 5. *Made for Him: God Uniquely Made Me for My Husband*

Printed in the USA
CPSIA information can be obtained
at www.ICGtesting.com
LVHW071950170923
758232LV00084B/813